UK
A Third World Country

(A Voter's View)
Vol 1

By
Julie Rothchild

UK A Third World Country

Author: Julie Rothchild

Copyright © Julie Rothchild (2026)

The right of Julie Rothchild to be identified as author of this work has been asserted by the author in accordance with section 77 and 78 of the Copyright, Designs and Patents Act 1988.

First Published in 2026

ISBN 978-1-83538-895-2 (Paperback)
     978-1-83538-904-1 (Hardback)
     978-1-83538-896-9 (E-Book)

Cover Design and Book Layout by:
    Maple Publishers
    www.maplepublishers.com

Published by:
    Maple Publishers
    Fairbourne Drive, Atterbury,
    Milton Keynes,
    MK10 9RG, UK
    www.maplepublishers.com

The views expressed in this work are solely those of the author and do not reflect the opinions of Publishers, and the Publisher hereby disclaims any responsibility for them. This book should not be used as a substitute for the advice of a competent authority, admitted or authorized to advise on the subjects covered.

A CIP catalogue record for this title is available from the British Library.

All rights reserved. No part of this book may be reproduced or translated by any form or by any means, electronic or mechanical, including photocopying, recording or by any information storage and retrieval system without written permission from the author.

CONTENTS

Introduction And Why 5

Pillars of Society Starting to Crack 9

    Economic 11

    Law & Order 11

    National Security 11

    Infrastructure 12

    Collaborative Culture 12

    Political System 13

Politicians – Lacking Competence & Accountability 15

    They really think you buy the BS 17

    Out of Touch – The Voting Dichotomy 19

    Left Right Left Right – Somewhere in the middle 22

    Lack of Trust in Politicians – do they pass the simple test. 28

    Celebrity status over doing the Job. 29

    Tax Weapon 30

    Independence 36

    Striking Britain 38

    Out of touch Political System 39

Your Local Gravy Train Council 45

    Wasting Your Money – news flash 46

    Death of the Highstreet 48

    Speeding, Road Safety and all that nonsense 49

The Good, the Bad and the Spineless- Pre 2024 Election 53

    Tall stories and fake promises 53

    How The Parties Shaped Up In England 54

    What a bunch to choose from 57

Immigration – National Self Harm 70

    Immigration agenda heats up 72

Illegals Get a Priority Pass 74
  So why are so many people fed up with the Illegals? 76
  Is anyone asking the right questions about Immigration? 77
  Laughable Stories – Gullible State – No Common Sense 79
  Impact of Immigration 81
  Stopping Illegal and Managing Legal immigration 82
  Snowballing Monster 85
  Legals Vs Aliens 86
No Law No Order 88
  CPS - Guilty until Proven Innocent 89
  Tip of the Iceberg 90
  Casino Court Room 96
  Lack of respect for the police 96
  In the courts 98
  Turning the law on its head 100
Cleansing of the UK Culture 103
  Out of sight out of mind 106
  Eco Numpties – Stop What 108
  The Four Horsemen plus Z and Z+ 110
  Patriotism Not Allowed 111
The Winner of the 2024 General Election was? 118
  New Kid on The Block 118
  A Little Comment About Brexit 128
Old Labour/New Labour/Just Labour = KeirCo 131
  The lefties run off crying – Trump effect 133
The UK's future State 138
  Along Came Kemi 142
Your Role – Take Action 145
Nobody 147
Take 2 149

Introduction And Why

Is Great Britain great anymore or is it simply sleepwalking into becoming a third world country? It's already third world in some ways. Just look around, the evidence is stifling. You may think that the UK is 'broken', for me that's an understatement. It is more in the gutter and heading rapidly for the sewer rather than broken. Many aspects of our lives are already painful, and things will only continue to deteriorate as the politicians of our time seek to benefit and promote their own agendas, ignoring the very people who voted for them and let us not forget, pay their wages. The pace of deterioration will depend upon, what damage Labour do now and who gets power in 2029. Whichever party gets in; it will not stop the rot. It is only a matter of time before we are at the bottom of the sewer asking the rest of the world to bail us out.

You may think that recent events like Covid or the cost-of-living crisis are easy things to point at and write about, and you would be right. However, that is only a small part of the story, as this country spirals out of control. There is a distinct lack of accountability from the pillars of our community, central government and the so-called trusted sources who should set the standards and lead by example. Good, solid, dependable role models, leaders, being proud and patriotic have almost disappeared, due to far-left being embedded in pretty much every government department. Yet the people in the street 'the good old taxpayers' are being tricked into silence. Suppressed and fearful, they are frightened to speak up for themselves in case the 'woke' and 'do-good community' object. The moral fibre of this once great country is being dangerously pulled to the far left – stagnation and decline are present in every aspect of our lives in the UK.

This book is not an attempt to put the country down; can it go much lower one asks? Look around you – oh yes, it can, I say. Wait and see. However, rather than rattle on like the opposition party or the strident do-gooder crowd, this book offers solutions to problems that would work. Although, some folk would deem them unpalatable, albeit necessary to stop the decay and the utter mess that the UK is.

The UK is being subjected to some weird political experiment by the governments old and new, local councils, civil servants, subliminal messaging via advertising. All are fuelled by the negative bias from some media agencies to the political left – not to mention the fake news brigade. The very culture, spirit and lessons learned from our history that made this a great, patriotic country may not be sufficient. A few years will pass and there will be a point of no return – mediocrity - liberalism will prevail, the rich will get richer, and the poor will get poorer. The middle class will disappear. The class system will become those with and those without and the untouchable rich and powerful 'The Elite'.

It is important to highlight the perpetrators whose cacophony of bad decision making, self-interest, personal agendas and total disregard for working people, need to be exposed. You may have read, watched and probably talked about many of the examples referred to in this book with friends, family and work colleagues. However, have you deciphered the code and real consequences? It is the culmination of events, toxic politics not isolated issues that have led the UK to this point. Turning this country around will be virtually impossible. Like a boxer, the UK continues to take political blow after blow with no time to recover. From this point on (this book is being published in the third final quarter of 2025) things in the UK will only get worse. The sleepwalking has started. Political systems and legal framework in the UK are out of touch with reality; politicians will continue to chase international agendas and celebrity status; the UK problems and citizens will simply be placed at the back of the queue; crime will continue to rise; big business will become more profitable and more controlling. Technology will be used to create a nanny state. The everyday persons in the street will have less money in their pocket to spend and far less freedom.

You the reader of this book still have power. More action is needed and that starts with you.

Julie Rothchild

Without Rules, Structure and Good Examples to follow we are no better than animals.

Pillars of Society Starting to Crack

The so-called pillars of society, provide a structure for how we go about our daily life, how we should behave and live in the UK. The pillars act as a map if you like of how to go about things in your life; work hard, get paid, save for your retirement, be law abiding, be respectful of others. In return, if you follow the map you should get to the expected destination. Yes, there will be challenges, but the map will also have laybys, rest and support areas, safety nets in case you need to pause your journey or take a different unexpected route. The foundations of the pillars are trust, honesty, reward for your efforts, perseverance and integrity, accountability and responsibility of those that set the guidelines and run the system.

Above the pillars are you and me, the public, citizens that have a rightful, legal place to be here in the UK. The system below should offer stability and certainty in return for you playing your part and following the rules. The pillars reward you, and you have a safe, happy and prosperous and contented life. However, since the mid to late nineties, the pillars have been crumbling (Blair, Coalition and Tories), the foundations and structure have been diluted. The results are there for you to see. Do you feel safe? Do you feel the state is looking after you? Do you feel happy and contented? Do you have enough money in your pocket to live without worry? The elite Left do, but the vast majority of the country will tell you a different story, not just financially but in many other ways.

At the base of the pillars are the foundations. The individuals who heavily influence it are either leaders or controllers. Many years ago, these were royalty and the church who established a map that should be followed for a good life. The map started to become mainstream in the UK between the Edwardian and Victorian era. Many say, the foundations were established for the gain and prosperity of the rich and powerful rather than the people of the time in the years between 1820-1914. Has much changed over the last 100 or so years considering where we are today? It is the Government who have held control of the pillars and foundation since the end of the 2nd World War in 1945 that have the most influence by which we live and navigate the map to-day in an attempt to achieve a harmonious and prosperous society. As political parties change and power shifts, so does the map. The more stable the map the more stable society is. During the period 1965 - 1990 we had leaders who lead by example had a strong moral compass, hard work ethic and accountability for their actions. Since then, we have had more controllers, who have failed to lead, have set no example and are more interested in left wing ideology and self-interest. So, the map, like the coned off and appalling road network in the UK has become very difficult, almost impossible to navigate and plan with any certainty or confidence in the society we experienced in the previous 10-20 years.

There are many definitions of what the pillars are. The current left wing has attempted its own definition of gender equality as an addition 'rather than treating everyone equally' - everyone meaning everyone (lefties running scared I guess) Personally my explanation of the pillars is more aligned to Maslow's hierarchy of needs and the five pillars of society. As you read through the book I will highlight why and who is responsible for the utter mess that the UK is. The pillars are:

Economic

A stable economy should be designed to benefit the citizens. Stability provides certainty and enables governments to plan - keeping interest rates in check and low inflation are key contributors. The main consideration, as with personal finance, is ensuring your costs are significantly lower than the money coming in so that you do not end up borrowing and paying interest. On a personal level, for the last 50 years or so we have been told to be prudent; save for a rainy day; get a pension so you will have money in retirement, and you will be rewarded. Those who have followed this path appear to be the ones now being targeted by Labour to prop up everyone else who has been careless with their money and have debt.

Law & Order

Protecting citizens with a fair and just Law & Order system is the hall mark of a good government. If justice is given fairly then it creates a more confident and trusting society. The public at large are generally accepting of the decisions the courts make on the understanding that there is a fair and honest trial. However, the public's trust has been significantly eroded due to the two-tier policing and political interference in the justice system, of which there are many examples. The system is being used as a sledgehammer to crack a nut and no one appears to be joining up the dots between crime, fair trial, prison capacity and rehabilitation. Locking people up that are not a risk to the public makes no sense. Is the Banksy message (Sept 2025) on the Royal Courts of Justice that far from the truth under Labour?

National Security

This is a subject that not many people understand or can comprehend, MI this and MI that and layers of Law and the state can do what we like if we choose to. Forget the double, triple agent, James Bond stuff. Yes, a lot of it is shrouded in secrecy. Will we or should we ever know what really goes on? To the citizen on the street, it is simple. Keeping the country safe, protecting our borders from potential or direct threats to our way of life internally or externally. I wonder if many people think we have the basics, right? Look at our unprotected coastline or supposed secure buildings, motorway gantries and military bases like Brize Norton. Secure doesn't spring to mind when they appear to walk in and just vandalise multimillion pounds of assets or just hop on a boat with no form of ID, just the latest smart phone, designer gear, and land on the beach at Dover.

Infrastructure

Adequate and efficient infrastructure to support us with travel, education, healthcare and emergency services et el. Ever tried going anywhere in the UK in a hurry? – thought so. Infrastructure is the fundamental framework of how we get things done in a country. There should be simple parameters put in place by the Government based upon simple data points like population growth, number of new motor vehicles, train travel, food consumption. This should drive infrastructure and be capacity based. It should set immigration targets based upon number of people per square meter. The UK ran out of capacity around 1980 - 1990 when the population was around 56 million (populationpyramid.net). Now we are at 70 million (satisticstimes.com) and growing fast so why haven't we invested correctly in a growing population and their needs?

Collaborative Culture

Having a collaborative culture does not mean we all have to like each other, more so, we should be accepting of other's beliefs and the way they go about their life. As long as everyone is treated equally and fairly and plays by the same rules, it works. If the pillars remain stable and the map is clear, this generally leads to improved conditions for everyone- all gravy, as they say. But is that the case in the UK? How do we treat the elderly? Why do we have unruly, 'don't give a crap' youth and a massive increase in crime and violence targeted towards each other?

Political System

A political system that is centred around favouring its own citizens as a priority over anything else. They should be responsive, strategic based upon the miles of data they have access to; they should plan and have strong experienced leaders. They should use these skills to predict future trends/outcomes and act before things get out of control and the pillars start to crumble. It is also about standing up for something, being clear and honest with the electorate, which shows their own strength. In recent times we have experienced poor leadership, more U-turns than ever before and individuals chasing celebrity status and on the international band wagon while the UK goes down like a sinking ship. What sort of example are these governments setting? All of this shows weakness, and having a spine is a pre-requisite for the job. The public can smell the stench – trust in politicians is at an all-time low.

For a society to function correctly and prosper all elements of the pillars need to be aligned.

Julie Rothchild

Like a magician on the stage trickery and misdirection is the name of the game - Politics

Politicians – Lacking Competence & Accountability

What is a politician? There are many definitions. Some I could quote, others perhaps not! There is a growing anger and animosity towards them and for very good reasons. They are public servants, the taxes you pay (and there are many and increasing by the minute) pay their salary, benefits, security, posh meals and other perks. Like a personal audience with Taylor Swift or hospitality boxes at special events to name a few. They get voted in (by You) and use taxpayers' money to keep the country going in whatever direction they choose. Depending upon who you choose, they are supposed to uphold your views and beliefs on everything from schooling, crime, laws, border control, the economy, public spending, cultural integration, defence and so on. The main qualities they need to have being trust, honest and integrity – they run the country after all and have control over your day-to-day life. The anger and animosity the public has is well founded. The problem with the UK is that politicians are too soft, bad decision makers and spineless. No one wants to make really difficult decisions (although that is the most common phrase in their handbook), in fact most of them make a career out of avoidance, not making those really difficult decisions and certainly not answering any questions in a truthful and honest way. In the last twenty years the game has been to play the middle ground in an attempt to please everyone, but in the end they please no one, other than themselves. Every decision they make can be supported by some research, adviser, expert, think tank, consultant and a totally convoluted thought process with not an ounce of common sense being applied. The overpaid Whitehall cronies (there are many of them) who support them have an answer and angle for everything – or at least that's what they think. Recent governments have been heavily reliant upon these so-called experts which says a lot about their leadership and ability to do the right thing. We pay billions £ of taxpayer's money to help politicians make a decision, many of these specialist advisors are all on daily rates of pay that most working people in the street can only dream of. If the decision makers in Government rely on the information from these sources, then why are the decisions and policies so reactive, rather than well thought through strategies? It seems to me that the knee jerk reaction we have seen over the last 10 years is more populist or embarrassment avoiding politics. What they fail to realise is that the voting public have heard it all before, it's the same old lies and bluster. So many lies and false promises over the decades! In the last ten years or so the public have grown tired of the bull shit and can see through it all, any trust and respect has gone. In my mind the voters have taken too long for this light bulb moment; if we had the same focus and perspective we have today, on politics 20-30, years ago the country might be in a better place than where we find ourselves currently.

Most of the voting public do not want a political party that is too far left or right. Somewhere nearer the middle is fine and sums up the majority of UK voting mentality. However, for the last 30 years under labour, conservatives and the coalition the UK has been headed way too far left and with Kier here in 2024 it will become extreme, with nanny state and socialist policies and tax hikes beyond your imagination. There are too many meddling privileged do-gooders and woketeers poisoning minds of the voters and some politicians in other parties. This, coupled with being spineless and self-centred politicians, it sums up the UK's political landscape at present. The impact and rate of deterioration has been and continues to be visible across the UK. There is a distinct lack of competence and accountability in the main parties which has simply filtered across all government funded departments, public services and local councils etc.

They really think you buy the BS

The current political strategy model is based on complete fantasy and lacks reality. The major parties have adopted the same old rubbish and expect you to suck it up and believe their unique selling points (USP). They base their policies and law in the same way. It's like the old-fashioned marketing department from the eighties selling pop records or cigarettes. Well now that marketing team has turned up in politics and it shows. It is all sell, sell , sell. All front - loaded headline grabbing and bold USPs, attract interest, just forget the back end and worry about it later; if and when something happens, we will blame the experts and the advice we had. All successful businesses consider the whole customer journey, the back end being implementation and delivery and ensure the upfront claims and promises made (sell) are actually achieved. Amazon, Microsoft, M&S have worked this out to a fine art. It is not just experiences it is common sense. Running the country is no different but now it simply lacks strong leaders with experience. As I have pointed out being a politician does not make you good at doing everything. There are plenty of companies who adopted the same strategy as the government; media, mobile network, utility and transport companies who fail to understand customer service.

So how does the political ideas generation model work? You would expect the core principle would be to prioritise the UK, for it to be based upon helping and meeting the voter's needs, giving to the public rather than just taking from the public. After all, you voted them in right. Well, the average voter has worked out that that is far from the truth. Big business, and the lobbyist spend millions of pounds trying to win favour with the government to ultimately gain more power over the man in the street and flog you a load of stuff you don't really need with a simple policy, regulation tweak here and there. The list of freebies goes on and on. Then the government have political commitments to keep like COP; G7 summit; saving the world from famine, space exploration, foreign aid. The justification for spending billions is that it keeps the UK on the world stage, (apparently) if you like keeping up with the Jones'. All this before they get to the UK agenda item – You the voter. To distract politicians even more we have 'what does the media have to say', 'what are the current topics we should be talking about'. Yes, even headline grabbing stupidity comes first.

There are many examples of this media grabbing, recently, of course is the post office scandal, the Blood scandal from 1970-1980 has gone quiet for now. Let us hope someone makes a new documentary out of that one, that will wake the politicians up. The governments past and present over the last 25 years have ignored the plight of the postmasters who lost their lives, homes and credibility. The well rewarded board of many politicians also ignored the facts. The action to rectify the utter wrongdoing has been incredibly slow and painful, adding further emotional blows to the victims (the Post Masters and their families). Yet when ITV make a drama to highlight the wrongdoing, Rishi Sunak, Keir Starmer and the political gang turn up like an unwanted rash to offer sympathy and help. It is a bit late really, the damage has been done by the political elite, grabbing the headlines and offering help and delivering justice and compensation, which translate to the average voter as, no real improvement or action will be taken to address the problem, all talk and no walk, but a nice little earner for their mates managing the compensation process.

Cutting $Co2$ is another example, tax incentives for all to get Joe public to change their habits. Electric car subsidies for all, heat pumps, free loft installation and more, the race is on to save the planet. It grabbed headlines alright; the UK were going to lead and show the world how amazing we were. In the rush to get a story out in the media (populist politics) they forgot some key fundamentals of infrastructure to support electric car and van charging. The cost of electric cars vs the normal combustion engine, who can afford an electric car even with the subsidy? Not many. And oh, we didn't realise heat pumps are on an average six times more costly than a conventional gas boiler. So why would the public rush to buy one? That scheme has failed. It is pathetic, and the good old tax payer ultimately picks up the bill for failure of these poorly thought through schemes. Not to mention the ridiculous amount of inconvenience people must suffer trying to find an electric charger for their electric car or being stuck in an electric car conga cue at a motorway service station (we have all seen them) when there are 30 cars waiting for 5 charging points. The harsh reality is that with all the consultants and advisors they still get the simple stuff badly wrong, because grabbing the headlines and celebrity status obviously means more. Where are the consequences for these schoolboy errors, we ask? The examples I have used are not even the complex or big policy change. They just require input from real people with competence.

Out of Touch – The Voting Dichotomy

When I vote I feel like I am always voting for the best of a bad bunch, there is no party that ticks all of the boxes, far from it. It feels like I must try and change something as the country is in the gutter, so I vote for the party I think can possibly delay or reverse the appalling downward spiral we are currently experiencing in the UK.

Watch the media strap lines trying to win favour with voters -it is so false. Populist politics is dangerous, if not just because it's short term, the here, the now, and is easily and conveniently surpassed by the next shiny big thing to take the headline, magpie management springs to mind. It demonstrates however a lack of leadership and long-term vision that this country needs in order to get us back out of the gutter. All this short termism and outright neglect for the voters' views from all parties gives me no sense of logic to turn up at the polling station. My decision to choose a party and put an X on the paper is based upon a party that represents 20-30% of my expectations – It is the best of a bad bunch. That's how bad politicians are at reading the mood of the nation and why people don't vote, especially the younger contingent. The last general election (2024) was a great example.

When looking at the leaders of the various parties the majority of them are so out of touch with the UK and what it is really like to live here - its laughable but actually very frightening. The insight and experience they have. How can anyone pass a policy or law that does not understand the real impact of their decision making on actual people? The vast majority of politicians are privileged, with wealth and privately educated. Many live in nice houses in nice areas and probably think anti-social behaviour, domestic crime and the cost-of-living crises are just myths. They have little or no experience of the struggles that the voting public living in the UK go through on a day-to-day basis. Do you think Rishi Sunak (Rishi), Keir Starmer (Kier) or the majority of their teams have to worry about their neighbours vandalising or stealing their property or living next door to a drug dealer who plays loud music at 2am in the morning? No. Or have they ever had to make a choice between putting food on the table or turning the heating on to keep warm in the winter like so many families and pensioners have to? No. Used a food bank? No. Or have they had their wife and children sneered and laughed at, shouted abuse at as they walk down the high street or corner shop where there are large groups of immigrant men hanging around? No absolutely not. The problem is they have read a book, passed an exam, but lack experience of what the UK has become.

The underlying issue is not just the leaders' backgrounds and their upbringing; it is very much the team they choose to surround themselves with, supporting their decision making – yep taxpayers' cash on consultants and Quangos. Many come from the same ilk, have the same perspective and privileged mindset. This is further complicated and agitated, (if you believe, The Plot by Nadine Dorries 2023, as I do), by the interfering senior civil servants that work in the shadows of Westminster with their own agendas. The political system that supports these individuals in setting and making decisions on Policy and Law, is also overly and deliberately complicated. The political system itself is broken and out of touch with the world we live in. The proof is so easy to see, we seem to be able to change tax laws and policy within a blink of an eye yet when it comes to the passing of the Rwanda bill; Asylum rules or changing EU Laws it is so slow – how many years is it since we left the EU and why are we still paying them? How come, sorting out government disasters like the Blood and Post Office scandal, not to mention changing the Immigration and Human Rights laws seems to take for ever? The answer to the question is simple it is about deliberate inefficiency, political self-interest, over doing what is morally right for the UK and its citizens. So many of the schemes the government put forward are deliberately complicated, flawed and unsuccessful. It is simply a regressive system, but no one has any interest in changing it. To make it worse the very people that use the system love to blame the system to cover their tracks and poor decision making. That perhaps is the reason why the Politicians and Civil Servants are reluctant and drag their heels when it comes to changing it. The current political system in the UK only benefits a certain set of individuals. Who you ask?

That said, it is important for everyone to vote and have an opinion, after all, it's your life and the folk in Downing Street and Whitehall have total control over it. As my mother would say 'If you don't vote you shouldn't discuss or have an opinion on politics' so have your say and **vote**. The issue I have is we always end up with a party that barely meets my agenda, overarching beliefs and values – does that sound familiar?

Left Right Left Right – Somewhere in the middle

The word 'extreme' thrown around by the media and politicians to highlight inappropriate behaviour is not a good one – But what about their behaviour? The majority of users sporting this phrase are far-left wing individuals. They use the word to label other people and groups who disagree with them. Rather than give a considered intelligent response to the right-wing views, they always throw in the word 'Extreme or Far Right' in a bid to totally discredit any challenge to their left-wing ideologies. The left go from DEFCON 5 (It is ok challenge me - Normal) too DEFCON 1 (you're a fascist/racist - Nuclear) as soon as you disagree; many just don't have a filter or really want to listen. It seems the left-wing views cannot be challenged; this attitude is blatant arrogance and elite behaviour. Disagreeing in the way of other people's views is itself extreme. A definition of extreme is 'largest possible amount or degree' or 'having such strong opinions that no one agrees with you' according to dictionary.cambridge.org. Or in real terms, if 0 was far Right and 10 was far left then both 0 and 10 would be extremes, 5 being in the middle ground.

The majority of sensible people like and appreciate balance and debate on this subject when free speech allows, ending somewhere in the middle. If we respect the basic principle of ' it is ok to have a view and a different opinion' and 'we are happy to debate our view peacefully' then people are accepting. We get on, we live and let live and we all prosper in so many ways. The issue today is that we are fed up with what we can't do - over controlled, overtaxed and our basic rights are challenged every day, free speech all but criminalised. The list appears endless, to top it all we seem to have an army of police officers and CPS more interested in prosecuting if you post a negative comment online let alone say it out loud in a pub or public place. People are saying 'police our streets not our tweets'. In short society and the authorities have forgotten it is ok to 'Agree to disagree'. Disagreeing with someone or something should be absolutely fine, it fosters acceptance and integration in society. However, the political interference and current stance on the subject of free speech has been driven by the Left-wing do-gooders and creating increasing divide within our society Perhaps we should go back to the nursery rhyme 'sticks and stone will break my bones, but names will never hurt me'. The modern version 'Knives and guns will kill me, but name calling will get me put in prison'. Wow, we have come so far.

The socialists, LibDems, labour and greens generally sit on the left, conservatives and reform sit on the right, although in the last 15 years the Conservatives have become more socialist and left wing in an attempt to appease the lefties and broaden their net for voters. This move will see Reform inappropriately branded as 'Extreme or Far Right' as the political playground bullies gang up on them as they start to gather pace, taking a bigger and bigger share of the vote in local and general elections. The far-right branding will be a desperate and deliberate attempt to deter and frighten moderate voters from taking a balanced view. Without political balance, maturity and accountability the UK will simply end up with the disgraceful and undemocratic situation that France found itself in. Macron's embarrassment at doing a poor job and contempt for the voting public led him into making an audacious move, by trying to foster a dirty deal with the Extreme left to keep out Marine Le Pen. I have discussed this topic with some French (voting) people and sense their considerable disdain for Marcon's antics. Revolution is in the air if the vote rigging does not stop in France, but let's just give a thought to Angela Rayners devolution plans to try and delay the local elections in May. Is that not tampering with voting? I genuinely feel that the voting citizens in the UK have had a skinful of the Conservatives and again Labour's continued U-turns, lies and antics. Lee Anderson's drive for more common -sense politics is badly needed in the UK, it's based more on transparency, truth and accountability – common- sense politics or just what politics should be, but not what it has become.

Unless you are using Extreme in terms of adrenaline sports, most extremes are not a good thing. Although even that depends on the level of mental and physical health you have before undertaking an extreme sport. But, whilst Extreme Right politics is bad, Extreme Left politics is a whole lot worse. Left wing views and idealism come from the wealthy and privileged who quickly discard views and living conditions of the man in the street. Left wing policies blur the governing lines and accountability. They remove basic rights; block free speech and debate; remove discipline, eroding levels of respect, which creates animosity, a social free for all, dog eat dog, don't give a crap environment - chaos quickly ensues, resentment takes hold and the people on the street start to turn on each other, whilst the privileged lefties sit up above the chaos like Cesar in the colosseum or gods in the clouds opining over the human disarray and squalor. Extreme left is 'Pure Elitism' and it's dangerous, yes, they support many chaotic activities, Just stop oil, Extinction Rebellion or the Transport Action Network are classic examples. The most common tactic used of course by the Left being to shout 'you're Far Right and a Nazi' if you disagree and do not share their views. These left-wing principles and behaviours can be witnessed on a daily basis all over the UK. It has not only taken a grip on a personal level it is in big business too, woke training and bias recruitment – no whites allowed here. The key question for all recruiters surely is whether you have the right experience, qualifications and attributes to perform the job. No, it appears to be based upon are you the right colour and gender to tick the box for the company recruiting so it can feel cosy, content and demonstrate conformity to the 'wokerati'. The copout to avoid criticism is the phrase Global Community, which appears to translate as 'not white male'. I have personally witnessed a very big company hold off giving the right candidate the job because a woman or person of mixed race had not applied. The white male I am referring to had to wait for three additional months whilst

Human Resources (HR) rushed around desperately to get anyone else rather than a white male. This is positive discrimination, but no one dare say anything or they would be bullied and sacked. Councils and pretty much every public service appears to be on EDI steroids, according to the taxpayersalliance.com there is enough of them. Around 700 roles costing approximately 40 - £50million a year; is that a good use of your council tax money, what benefit? What about weekly bin collection instead or fix the potholes? Open your eyes and look around, the public sector is ridden with this nonsense and expensive overheads adding no value. Unfortunately, many of the woke left contingent lack a spine. A lot of this recruitment appears to be done on the quiet. If I am wrong about the woke recruitment, why use colour and gender as a conditional requirement for public sector jobs on the advertisements? It implies that these criteria are more important than performing the job. Are there many people out there who are happy with the public sector performance?

So, in true form, from the Monty python film The Life of Brian (1979) 'what did the Romans ever do for us' since the prosperous times under a true right-wing government of Magaret Thatcher for example. Let's explore the benefits of what the left wing woketeers have given us. I count the last 15 years conservative rule as also being more aligned to the left rather than right. The conservatives have been hedging their bets to appeal to a wider electorate. Well, the list of benefits is lengthy, but not exhaustive:

- Knife crime and death of young people overall has increased
- Anti-social behaviour is at an all-time high
- Increase in number of violent incidents against teachers, ambulance drivers, NHS workers and the fire service
- Work shy workforce, mass progression of Gen Z and plus Z, most of whom are ill mannered, socially inept.

- More health and safety nonsense choking efficiency and progress.
- Society has more individuals than ever before with self-interest, entitlement at the top of the agenda.
- A shocking lack of respect in society in general, especially towards the elderly
- A country overrun and at crisis point with illegal immigrants, who consume more taxpayers' money than you can imagine.
- An out of control and biased legal system based upon points scoring rather than truth and justice for the people.
- Drug related crime and usage off the Richter scale in every town and city
- A country unable to control its own borders.
- Police no go/ don't go areas in many cities.
- Protesting and rioting in our streets for issues that are not related or of benefit to the UK, but are somehow allowed.
- A country that can hardly defend itself in a conventional war against anyone. Let us hope the illegals don't get tooled up and try and take us on our own turf.
- Politicians more interested in grabbing headlines rather than doing the job they are paid to-do.
- Poor performing economy, lack of any long-term financial stability.
- Crises ridden public Services/NHS who appear to be more interested in delivering EDI to its own work force than services to the public.
- An EDI agenda seems to have created more animosity and division in communities rather than a fairer and harmonious society.

- Cultural division, lack of integration of immigrants into UK culture
- Record number of homeless, especially children and veterans.
- Many hard-working legal immigrants heading back to their own country.

Yes, left wing politics and policies supported by the woke agenda have given us so much, eh. The structure, boundaries, discipline and respect have all but disappeared but look at what we have achieved. The UK establishment has stalled, and it is going backwards, it is simply not progressing.

Socialist left Labour doesn't like achievement, success or positive outcomes for individuals or the private sector business. They want to control everything ensuring that all roads lead back to the state. Tax rather than promote or blend together an open free market principle. Labour will take us too far in the wrong direction. Socialism and Far Left agendas are rarely successful, especially when you have the economic dynamic of more people taking out of the system rather than putting in. On a personal level, the more people who are employed by the state, are paid by the state, the more public sector departments, the more control they have over the key services. The last thing the UK needs is a Nanny state with all roads leading to the Government, but that's where its heading. Their track record of delivering anything to time or budget, other than tax hikes, is appalling.

So, Far Right is also undesirable, but what I see in our society in the UK is certainly not close to extreme or far right wing, more a step or two from the centre. Nigal Farage (Reform Party) might be a little more pro-Israel rather than Hamas, who shouldn't be? But does that make him 'extreme or Far Right' no! Nigel doesn't want mass cultural cleansing or concentration camps; he just wants order; structure; clear and defined boundaries; a respectful trusting and prosperous society. What the left hate is what is at the very centre of Reforms mandate, which is serving the majority of people in this country and their views – putting the UK citizens first, and not focusing on every other Tom, Dick or Harry's business and grovelling to the minority group of the population and Europe. After all democracy is about looking after the majority who should be prioritised, then addressing the rest. The lefties need to understand that since Blair was in power, the UK has fallen off the world stage, globalisation is yesterday's news. The western world is in such a mess that more and more countries are battening down the hatch and sorting out their own patch with issues similar to the ones in UK, before trying to solve everyone else's issues and problems. Just look at Europe and how great it's going there. Yes, Europe like the UK is suffering because of lazy left-wing politicians, with a lack of planning for the future and the majority, simply focusing on the wrong issues. The lefties are in a desperate place; their time is running out to show that the left-wing ideology have any signs of positive contribution to our society. They really need to stop shouting out 'You're Far Right' at anyone who doesn't agree with them, wake up instead take a good long look in the mirror at the so-called achievements and the mess the UK is in today.

Lack of Trust in Politicians – do they pass the simple test.

Trust is a simple concept. However, fostering and achieving trust in someone or an organisation has become increasingly difficult in the recent times. Everything is laid bare by social media in an instant for all to see. Hero one minute, cast aside demon the next. The core principle of trust, however, remains the same. If you say something and deliver to your word you start to gain trust, the more times you repeat and deliver your promise the trust increases. Trust is at the core of a person or organisation's integrity; without it, it is a downward trend, and no one really wants to be associated with you. In politics the outcome is simple, no trust, then popularity starts to fade, votes dry up and your last weeks' best friend/colleague stabs you in the back for someone more popular, potentially more trustworthy – now that would be refreshing!

Being on the front of the paper or on the news as a party leader does not buy you trust. What the public want is for the political system and the politicians to deliver on their promise. A great example is the Tory machine saying enough is enough, we will stop the Boats, funny that the boats are still coming, the numbers seem to be increasing by the day, they certainly will under Labour-trust me. It is very easy to see why the public at large have no trust in politicians. The only PM in recent years, love him or loathe him, was Boris during the Covid outbreak. He did many great things under a truly challenging set of circumstances, although he went and shot himself in the foot with Partygate and all the contradictive messaging to the people on the dos and don'ts and then he got rumbled. On the trust front his party should have stepped in and tried to recover the situation, rather than a public knifing in the back. It could have been dealt so much better than the pre-school play - ground antics we so often see. Trust again is eroded by such churlish behaviour.

Celebrity status over doing the Job.

Whatever the media pump out as headline stories, a politician is not that far behind with a comment. It would seem that these days politicians see themselves more as celebrities rather than individuals who should lead by example and be accountable for their decisions. Instead, they take every opportunity to get their mug (face) or voice and opinion in the media and the media love it. The story that gives them limelight wins the day and the PM, the hangers on and opposition all jump on the band wagon to try and solve the problem and get airtime. I am sure if someone did analyse the amount of time politicians appear in the UK media in the last few years, they would be in the top 10 over any given year, especially in the election year. The media buzz word/quote of recent times is to say, 'We had difficult decisions to make'. This must be the most overused phrase in the political vocabulary to deliver bad news, they have no idea what a difficult decision is, but they think just by saying it, it is a justification, and they can feel vindicated. I appreciate that the media is an effective way to get messages across, but how refreshing would it be for a politician to give us some good news or even better they deliver on their promises. I am certain that the advisers say to politicians get your mug in the media and it will increase your popularity. This is a lie, it might increase familiarity with names to a face, nothing more. It is not as if the viewing public like seeing politicians on TV because they do talk a load of rubbish, most people simply turn over or turn off. I would like to see a politician deliver to their promises, set a good example and sort the country out and stop trying to compete as a celebrity.

Tax Weapon

There are only two sure things in life 'DEATH and TAXES'. Death is inevitable it comes in many forms, is often painful and evokes emotional despair. So, it's almost identical to tax! The current tax collar the people of the UK have around their neck is stifling; we are all suffering. The trend is alarming; in 2023/2024 the UK was suffering the highest tax burden on record according to the Daily Express online (30/01/24). The current levels of tax are the highest they have ever been in (2024/25). There is more pain to come in the next few years as Labour bleed everyone dry - the so-called wealthy; car driver; independent businesses; pensioners and hard-working persons. Yes, the one-trick-pony Labour will simply weaponize the tax system. As we head to the Autumn statement 2025, I suspect we all know that we will be burdened with greater taxes, in one form or another.

Governments in the UK deploy tax like a weapon on UK citizens to collect cash and fill the treasury coffers, spending it as they see fit, illegal immigration stampede, education, NHS, housing, defence, universal credit and so on. In recent years taxes have increased to their highest. The main philosophy being - we have spent more than we thought, so let us tax more, taking more from the people (you). You may think that only working people are taxed, but this is simply not true. Everything you buy from groceries, fuel, insurance, a house, going on holiday, a car and energy to heating your home, these all have some form of direct, in-direct or stealth tax attached to them. The only exception I can find is children's products, however both the transport of these goods to the retailer, and the production costs to make these items in the UK or elsewhere are taxed and factored into the overall cost you pay at the till. There are the direct taxes you will know, income tax, corporation tax, council tax, the shameful inheritance tax etc. However, there are other forms of taxation, that I call lying or trick tax. These are taxes that pretend to be for a specific issue like Road tax. Yet the money doesn't get spent on the roads, let alone the pothole epidemic, not to mention the ULEZ tax/charge Sadiq Khan introduced. What clean air initiatives? The funds however just go into the London Mayor's coffers to spend on his personal projects. The BBC TV licence tax/charge is another one, were does the money go? It's clearly not on the TV programmes, another tax and waste of money.

Inheritance Tax is shameful; it's no surprise that it is the most hated tax in the UK. You spend your whole life paying tax on everything, whatever you have left when you die is then taxed again if you fall into the threshold which will get lower and lower. Banks and other financial institutions assist in the process of helping the government by imposing costly probate services, so you have to justify and prove you are entitled to anything you may have been left by a loved one. In turn, if you fall into the process/tax threshold, the good old tax man is informed automatically, and he will be watching you. Quite frankly this is a disgusting and immoral tax, which all politicians should be ashamed of. The Daily Telegraph and others have campaigned to abolish it but to no avail. The simple reason is the tax raises too much money £5-7bn a year, and there isn't a chancellor out there bold enough (make a difficult decision) to abolish it. The percentage we pay will increase and the thresholds for paying it will decrease catching more people in the net. A bit like the NHS reducing the blood sugar test to catch diabetes earlier, I wonder why more people have it now. You work all your life, pay tax - tax strike 1; with the remainder you pay your bills that also have tax added to them (fuel duty/VAT) etc - tax strike 2; you prudently save for a rainy day with what you have left you try helping other family members, then die and it's not just the grim reaper that comes for you it's the tax man, wanting a third slice of tax - tax strike 3. Seems to me that tax man and the grim reaper are interchangeable in this context.

I will not pretend to be a tax expert, as taxing in the UK has been deliberately made complex to catch out the unaware. HMRC always tells you what you must pay but is reluctant to provide tips to mitigate any tax burden. However, as a taxpayer, I will offer you my opinion on why and how we are taxed in the UK and offer a simple explanation.

Core principle - The more you tax people the less they have to spend, so debt increases at a personal and business level, this is bad for the economy again highlighting a lack of forward thinking from government. An economy will stagnate, grow slowly for two reasons:

- ✣ Public spending/government bills (including interest on debt) too high and out of control - more tax needed.
- ✣ Lack of disposable income – all industries/businesses start to suffer promoting slow growth – more tax needed.

If you cannot control the bills or structure what is being spent in Government correctly, then the chancellor simply passes their poor money management issues onto the public. Growing economies need more disposable cash to spend so industry, retail, services and manufacturing grow creating more jobs. Gross

Domestic Product (GDP) increases, and lower inflation and stable interest rates provide stability. Most folk in the UK have a far less disposable income/stability since Covid and have had to cut back because of the 'tax on everything' mantra and government's inability to control inflation, interest rates and their bills.

The answer seems simple, why is the government not controlling its spending better rather than just throwing taxpayers' money around like a kid in a candy shop? The biggest money pits are the NHS, Civil Service and the crack pot pet projects (HS2/ Cardon Capture/millions more houses) to name but a few who give little or no return for their investment. How can the NHS be allowed to employ so many people that have little or no patient contact? Why do we have senior EDI (woke) managers and Finance Directors (bean counters) on six figure sums? The people that are running many of the trusts/hospitals are not leaders and don't have good business acumen, when did they have to make or sell something to make a profit? Their role is to take the money from the government; employ a few people; negotiate a few contracts (ineptly I might add) and spend it. That's simple stuff. Such roles should be minimised, their contracts simplified and with much lower pay scales applied. In fact, the only decision they do make is how much the parking fees go up. Ripping off the public a bit more for seeing their loved ones in need of help (this obviously excludes Scotland as they get parking for free). Paying £200K - £300k for this type of role is mind boggling stupidity and unnecessary. Millions of pounds could be saved in culling these roles quickly. It was so good to see the Daily Mail (26/5/25) run an article on NHS Fat Cats. We have all suspected these ridiculous rates of pay, however there are nearly 300 people on more than £200k a year. The article highlighted pictures of the greedy individuals all on over £300k a year. Surely Wes Streeting the Health Minister should be asking questions. Would he know what to ask? Amazingly we are paying these individuals top private sector money yet not one of them runs a hospital that is in the top 10 waiting lists on A&E. This implies to me that their contract of employment needs a good overhaul considering performance measures like; waiting lists; number of complaints; patient death rates etc. Top money, poor performance what a job, where do I apply?

The civil servants based in Whitehall and their unaccountable quangos should also be streamlined. Would a 50% reduction in their numbers make any difference to the 'so called' value they add? We all know the answer to that question, don't we? Well, it should be implemented. They are overpaid, strike happy and consistently underperform whilst working from home. If you believe the gov.uk numbers reported in the Daily Mail (24/3/25) why on earth does the Ministry of Defence need 2480 individuals in Finance, or the Ministry of Justice need 1170 personnel in human resource. I have worked for global organisations and big businesses in the UK for many years and have never seen such numbers of support staff employed, what a bloated state the UK has become. When we finally do get rid of them, (and its very rare-it's the old boys club), they get gold plated payouts and pensions, while everyone else who loses their job gets the statutory minimum. One must question the moral compass of these individuals who struggle to turn up to work and complete a full week. They preach that everyone should go back to work, but they are the last to conform. They are clearly taking their working cues from the politicians in Westminster. This will only get worse now that our Labour friends are in the driving seat. Yes, the number has not reduced, instead it has increased significantly, more jobs for their mates, loaded with hypocrisy. Since the introduction of zero-hour contracts in 2015 the British worker is considerably worse off. There is a distinct lack of loyalty from employers and employees alike, that's why the service industry in the UK is so, so bad. Angela Rayner's socialist workers review will only make the job market worse; handing most of the power to workers is counterproductive. The cost of producing pretty much anything will increase for the public – great move Angela! Companies will think twice about recruiting – less jobs for people, more AI and automation and the quality of goods will deteriorate to try and hold the price. We have all witnessed chocolate bars and bags of crisps getting smaller, with the advertising claim of holding or keeping costs low. The workers review after all is being pushed on us by someone who has never really had a job outside of the public sector. Angela has worked and supported the unions and has a very poor view of the private sector, let alone comprehend how businesses make a profit.

Billions could also be saved by stopping illegal immigration, the freebies and red-carpet treatment they get on arrival; pointless public inquiries like 'Chilcote' that are just jobs for the boys and we all know Tony lied, with no consequences. It was a pointless waste of money – how much (£10million) and how long did it take (7 years – what a joke), and the important questions is what value did it add to the public? What about the extreme levels of red tape we are paying for to compensate for a massive miscarriage of Justice in the post office scandal? – Have the 900 or so post masters been paid yet – probably not, remember when politicians are involved it will take for ever. Why are we sending money to other countries who clearly have bigger and better economies than us – India springs to mind. Yes, international aid or canning the topic has been around for a long time in the last 20 years, a lot of talk and bluster, very little action.

The list of waste in government is endless, but no one in government wants to make really difficult decisions do they? If you want to find billions of pounds look under the mattress in No 10, rather than chasing the media spotlight, G7, COP any other excuse not to sort out the UK. There is a simple principle that politicians need to adopt, as my mother would say 'before trying to sort everyone else's problems out, make sure your own house is in order first'. In translation – focus on this country and its people's problems and help us prosper, taking some of the pain away, before wasting and giving away money to everyone else. However, we must remember that a typical trait of a politician is to take the least line of resistance which isn't difficult.

Independence

The Scots have for many years pushed the subject of an independent Scotland, the rhetoric from Alex Salmon and again with Nicola Sturgeon, however the people of Scotland appear to be divided. I have many Scottish friends, I have worked and stayed in Glasgow and Edinburgh for many a year, and I struggled to find anyone that wanted independence or anyone that even liked Nicola. It would seem that, yet again, the politicians appear to follow their own agenda and have forgotten how and why they were voted in. Now Wales are in the fray for independence 'Yes Cymru' and their cronies say the time is right and they can break away as they have financial stability. The BBC ran an article on this in Jan 2024 suggesting that an independent Wales's option was viable, but as with these types of report they leave little or no firm way of how it would be achieved, more political rhetoric.

Some Welsh politicians are also toting the possibility of having their own currency and central bank. According to callingengland.co.uk (Feb 2024) I do wonder who they will have on the first coin or note, perhaps Tom Jones or a member of The Senedd to celebrate the hated introduction of the 20mph speed limit in Wales. Apparently, businesses and many locals objected to this, and some limits were changed back, after a considerable amount of money was wasted. Speed limits are one thing but, my worry would be letting the same politicians vote for independence and lead their country into bankruptcy rather than prosperity. Time will tell.

Then there is Northern Ireland, which despite the divide and difference in the region, appears to be happy with the UK as it is for the moment, perhaps due to the constant influx of funding like Wales and Scotland receive from England, so they should be careful what they wish for. At least Northern Ireland seem to be thankful and try to make a difficult political situation work. There is talk of a united Ireland - the joining of North and South. To me this could be a good and viable option as they share the same land mass, the biggest barrier being the European Government who are desperate to hold on to any country that has their currency and abides by their draconian Pro-European left-wing ideology. Southern Ireland leaving or Northern Ireland joining will be an interesting future debate.

Personally, I think if the people vote, democracy prevails and either the Scottish, Welsh or Northern Ireland people should leave, then it is all good. However, they do so at their own risk. The main one being how they manage their own purse, which has been topped up by England since the UK was established. It's a bit like Nicola Sturgeon telling the Scottish they could survive on the North Sea oil revenue, an economy based upon a volatile oil market which is playing school-time budgeting. If the oil price is high then great, but when it drops or when the market flatlines as it has done before and does so often, Scotland would have been bankrupt overnight. Again, it demonstrates politicians promoting their own agenda and going celebrity with rhetoric, rather than well thought through strategies or indeed representing the views of the people that put them into the position of power to create financial stability and prosperity. The political wet dream or key dimension that is constantly brushed under the carpet every time the topic of independence raises its head, is the expectation that England will keep paying. The answer to this wet dream should be far less emotional and patriotic if Westminster had a spine. The response should be 'please leave and when you do the funding will stop immediately'. The day they leave, no financial umbilical cord attached for years and years to come – sod off. However, how likely is it that common sense in Westminster would prevail? What has the track record been like over the last 30 years? Ask yourself this. We left the EU five years ago (in 2020) but we continue to give them millions of pounds of your hard-earned money and it's not likely to stop any time soon. The people voted in a democratic way to 'Leave' yet the politicians are still dancing around their handbags in Brussels sucking up to an unelected parliament to gain some form of political kudos and favour. The good people in the street get the message about the distribution of wealth and financial investment across the whole of UK, but not all of it is fair though it generally works, so why are politicians so dumb and inept at telling the truth about independence? Headline grabbing and arrogance springs to mind.

Striking Britain

Strikes across the UK, train drivers, nurses, doctors, ambulance, it is not wrong to have your say and ask for more.

Broadly, the public support the nurses; the care and hours they put in has long been unappreciated by every government. They have relied on the good spirit and passion of the individuals who choose a nursing career. It's not a surprise that many nurses leave that career and end up taking a second job to make ends meet or take a supermarket job and that pays more per hour. My mother was a nurse and died in her 80's still a nurse. It was the passion to care, help and love for people in general. As the core carers for the community at large, it a disgrace how they are treated. The nail in the coffin is how much some of the new woke jobsters and NHS bosses earn for going nowhere near the patients and taking the majority share of the money given to them by the taxpayer, what value do these people add to the patient? Zero.

The ambulance personnel fit into the same category as the nurses although what is worse for these folk (from the research I did) is that many of these exceptional individuals are on zero rate contracts, yet their bosses remain on cushy contracts. The biggest question for the government and the Ambulance Services is how do you create commitment, loyalty and a sense of belonging with someone who is on a zero-rate contract? Simple, you take advantage of their good nature.

Junior doctors I have slightly less time for. yes, they play a vital role, but many of them earn good money, the issue with pay caps on additional hours and earning is total nonsense, but it's the same for everyone who is lucky enough to earn £60 -100K a year- not just doctors. The more qualified doctors avoid these issues and push additional income through their Ltd companies or partnerships on private work to minimise the tax burden legally. Junior payroll doctors have less flexibility. I do think they should get more; however, asking for a 20% increase is totally unrealistic given the current job landscape (2024/25).

As for train drivers and rail staff, in general. they deserve nothing, they earn enough for what they do and contribute. Perhaps I am oversimplifying it but driving a train along a fixed track from A to B and following instructions like the highway code or a call centre clerk reading off from a screen is hardly difficult. The rail industry, since good old British Rail, has been plagued by over obsessive unions and a lazy work force, that has been happy to join in the rally for chaos and are not good people. I am all for people getting a fair deal, but what bothers me most is, (I have had firsthand experience of) is the immense impact striking has on normal hard -working people, many of them earning a lot less than train drivers. It causes massive inconvenience to hard working people many losing their jobs because they cannot get to work; many family trips ruined and the massive cost to the economy. The overall issue with the rail network is manifold, it would be nice if they actually ran on time.

The problem is that when you give into them with no strings attached, they will just keep coming back for more. Not to worry though, the politicians will sort it out – it won't be long before they start striking again!

Out of touch Political System

The political rot and self-interest have and will remain in place if it is left to the existing parties (Labour, LibDems, Greens,

SNP) and senior Whitehall cronies and agitators. They know no different, it's what they are used to so why change anything? The country has lapsed into political chaos (some say squalor) does anyone know who or what they are really voting for anymore? So little differentiation, lack of true leaders, example setters and U-turn after U-turn, is the norm. Then they do the dirty washing in public fighting with each other like children in the playground, these people run the country you know – Wow. What is needed to get this country back on track is either Reform or a re-energised post-Rishi Conservative Party that puts the people in this country first not every other country/minority. We know politicians love a few air miles, but we need to stop wild global money-pit initiatives that deliver nothing back to the UK. Self-interest, personal agendas and media point scoring, chasing celebrity, definitely needs to stop; strong leadership is required, not the constant self-pity because you apparently had to make a 'difficult decision'- it's part of the job darlings. A decision is not difficult or tough when it can be made and implemented at the drop of a hat, that's called a 'Choice' and a choice to do so whether it's well thought through or not. An example being it's not difficult, it is indeed very easy to tax people on emissions/carbon output, it's even easier to remove the heating allowance from pensioners. What would be difficult and tough would be; taking on the world's biggest polluters, China, India or the USA in the international court (which is a useful excuse when you need one).Or putting in place real sanctions against them because of the level of pollution they create; or culling the Whitehall cronies or EDI directors across the public sector and not robbing those already in fuel poverty and on the breadline. The interesting thing about climate control (depending on whose analysis you refer to) is that the UK does not even fall into the top twenty world polluters! Why then is our government (labour) so obsessed with punishing the taxpayer to support crack-pot energy schemes that drive prices up?

That's the poor behaviour addressed, but how we vote and how the country is structured politically to deliver real change, generate prosperity in the form of better standards of living is probably the difficult part to achieve:

<u>Introduce Mandatory voting</u> for all eligible folk but give them the opportunity to put their X on a vote of no confidence too. I have voted but I do not believe any of the parties are offering what I want. So, the right to abstain should be recorded. Another option would be to extend the voting window for four days over a weekend, not everyone can make the polling station or have access to a postal vote, some people do have day jobs and have to pay tax. The vote of 'no confidence' would be a lot more popular than you think and should be promoted to drive real change to the current spin machine that consistently fails to deliver. It would certainly send a message to the political elite dancing around their handbags, wining and dining on your money, that you as a voter are not impressed by this and their performance is well below par.

<u>Consequence and Accountability Board</u> for all government personnel. It should not be chaired by any of the political set but be truly independent. Like all good companies measuring performance is key, but politicians dodge this like the plague – I wonder why? For far too long politicians have been marking their own homework. Politicians should be held to targets; this would help them moderate their behaviour and stop them opening their mouths so quickly and over promising. It might also get them to think, analyse and ask smarter questions about the data they are given. There should be consequences, you fail and you're out or you're not getting paid for a year. It should also address the appropriate use of taxpayers' cash on their expenses, big meals, air travel etc and a serious challenge, did it add value to the country or was it just a joy ride. Politicians and civil servants need to be sacked like any other failing working individual, and a clawback system put in place on their salary/perks if they do not adhere to

the rules or targets. The dodgy pay offs and deals done behind closed doors need to stop, it simply erodes trust in the system.

<u>A split political system</u> to address day to day running and one to one focus on Infrastructure.

One should focus on the country's more immediate need with basic duties that are short term - 2-4 years to implement. This day- to- day government should focus on the Tax, law & order, punishing big corporates who rip off the public, i.e. Insurers, oil and gas companies and other utility companies who have done little to re-invest rather than profit grab, those who make absurd/record profits but claim the markets are tough and say the customer has to pay the price. And in particular, a bug bear of mine, ombudsmen and regulators who always seem to rule in favour of the business that pays their salary, so it's no surprise why they are ineffective. The biggest focus should be on streamlining and improving the Public Services and removing the waste that sits within it; that does not mean employ countless more expensive consultants and useless government committees to manage it, we all know how well it went at the Post Office.

The second would be an Infrastructure Government that would address long term - 4–15-year- strategy to ensure the country's infrastructure is adequate for the challenges the country faces. This should be easy given the stats/reports, data points that are available to them to predict future trends such as population growth and demographics on age, roads usage. This should set a list requirement to address potholes, railways systems and large-scale building projects, hospitals, prisons and schools. However, the Government must get rid of the mates' club, jobs for the boys and employ people that have expertise, experience and a track record of delivering and managing large complex issues, not too many politicians or civil servants at the table for that matter, but a mix of people with skills and common sense to sort the infrastructure out. That definitely does not mean individuals who have had government contracts before.

The biggest challenge would be getting the split system to work, it would require leadership, collaboration and a focus on the UK. As evidenced above these are not skills or behaviours that politicians appear to have.

Winning back the trust is so simple, stop lying, get a spine, make and take on real difficult and tough challenges, 'make those really difficult decisions – grow a pair'. Do your job and start prioritising the UK people over everyone else.

Julie Rothchild

Tax goes up, services deteriorate - We Love wasting your hard-earned money

Your Local Gravy Train Council

Your local or county council are there to provide a service for you the residents of a particular community. Reports in the Independent (20/2/24) and the Mirror (18/2/24) online suggest that the majority of them are suffering some form of financial difficulty and will push the Council Tax rise to the maximum, some have even asked to go above the cap set by the Government. We should be getting a reduction or refund given the terrible services most of us receive. Bin collections have been reduced; many areas have to pay garden tax to have the grass cuttings and garden waste collected. The councils continue to take more money and reduce the services to the community.

There are many reasons cited for their failure but in summary, it's bad financial management. Probably either poor management of service contracts or investing in expensive schemes that are poorly thought through, many of which residents don't want or didn't ask for. They will simply say like they always do – we did a public consultation - don't blame us. You must remember that the council employ people to manage their services and budgets, they also have tons of information and statistics to foresee upcoming issues to enable them to manage their coffers. Blaming population growth or aging population or the cost of care is incompetence. So, what on earth have they been doing - clearly not their job, they are perhaps too pre-occupied with how they reduce their already part time hours, four- day week further, or opining on all the mandatory woke and EDI training they do. The financial woes are not limited to recent times; the bad management has been going on for years. Whilst the political party overseeing the councils may change from year to year, the employees and management very rarely change, they just plod on. There are many examples of their failings to be seen in local and national media. There are a worrying number of bankrupt or insolvent councils; Birmingham, Woking, Northampton, Croydon and Slough to name a few. Bradford, on the brink, according to the Yorkshire Post online (06/01/24) and there will be many more. If I ran a company or organisation the way they do, I would be totally embarrassed and resign. However, the folk that run the councils are not unlike politicians and go deaf to problems and hope they go away or try and hide their incompetence. Councils simply lack accountability to you the taxpayer, heads need to roll.

Wasting Your Money – news flash

Councils don't often get it right. The most hated word in the vocabulary of the council will be 'maintenance' - upkeep of services to the community. Look at the footpaths, roads, shopping areas, overgrown bushes and trees and how they care for the elderly, the list goes on. A few examples:

Hampshire - GB news (Feb 2024) reported that Hampshire County Council had undertaken a £20m round- about project to improve traffic in the Basingstoke area. It was so badly laid out with poor signage, motorists and pedestrians have complained about the scheme calling it dangerous, confusing and a waste of money. It wasn't perfect before the so-called improvements, how could they make it worse? Councils use planning tools to map the layout of such projects, however this time common sense should have prevailed. I am sure they will blame the computer for the mistake rather than be accountable and sack the people who came up with the scheme and approved it.

York - The York press (5/1/2023) reported the stupidity of York Council wasting £8m of taxpayers' money on replacing a fleet with electric vehicles and hiding them away because they are unable to charge them. This is clearly a procurement issue and the vehicles were ordered in 2020, however, rather than try to renegotiate the contract they simply took delivery and stored them in a field hoping no one would notice. You would have thought that someone would have used common sense and planned charging points before taking delivery. Whilst York promotes EV charging, it got this one completely wrong. Rather than use the £8m, improving services to residents and adding value – free parking maybe? What this demonstrates is a poorly thought through scheme, after all it's not the council's money it's yours, the taxpayer's.

Isle of Wight - On the Isle of Wight the Medina estuary separates East and West Cowes. For years there has been a chain ferry referred to as the floating bridge. The local council have continued to mess around with it as a pet project, and it was replaced at a cost of £3.5m seven years ago. Unfortunately, now yet again, it will need to be replaced as the new floating bridge has suffered recurring problems and achieved 40% less performance than the old one, that local residents did not want it replaced. Now extra money will need to be found to buy a new one, that money could be spent on much needed services to the community that so desperately need it. Let's hope the council pick a better design this time around, rather than waste taxpayer money again.

In London - GB News online (18/3/24) reported that councils are spending over £50m a year on woke initiatives (EDI). What's the benefit to the taxpayer I ask? This is crazy when you think how bad the public services are to taxpayers. Another example of ignoring common sense and wasting your money. If you think that's bad how about the home office celebrating World Hijab Day as reported in the Daily Telegraph online (9/02/24). It would seem stupidity knows no bounds. Again, it's only your money they are wasting. How about spending the money helping the elderly?

Oxford - There's the one about the £51m car park left empty. Apparently, Oxford County Council and the highways agency failed to talk to each other as there is no funding for the road to join the car park to the main carriage way. It seems, it was a timing issue that created the problem. More like it's time to issue some P45s.

Plymouth - Armada way used to be such a nice place; then the Council one evening came along against the public will and massacred hundreds of trees, leaving the shopping area like a war zone, reported the Daily Mail (16/3/23). According to the Council they will spend millions of taxpayer's monies on something that no one wanted. Like Sheffield Council who were found to have acted dishonestly when it felled swathes of healthy trees.

Death of the Highstreet

This is clear for all to see. The obvious signs are the outbreak of charity shops; charity beggars (those who ask for your banking details rather than cash); more estate agents; more coffee shops, and more barbers. (I do wonder where the money comes from to fund an establishment that can survive on two haircuts a day). The emergence of the Turkish barber started in 2022, but don't worry, the tax man and crime fighters have only just woken up in 2025 and are investigating foul play and anti-money laundering – better late than never. It's bizarre that the council didn't spot it after all the internal training they do. So, all these establishments are replacing traditional retailers, and many more shops are being boarded up with people sleeping in the doorways; they are clearly not illegal asylum seekers. There is an increase in generally dirty and poorly kept seating areas and facilities, and of course pedestrianisation in the name of good old health and safety. These pedestrian areas are so poorly policed it's a joke, although if safety was a real issue why do I have to dodge bicycles, Deliveroo riders and e-scooters on a regular basis while walking down a pavement, let alone a high street. The riders have so much attitude and contempt for pedestrians, yet go un-challenged and unprosecuted, I guess it's too much to ask of the council or police to do their job. Does that sound like a place near you?

The death of the high street is the chosen strategy for most councils who want to turn them in to entertainment zones with boring chain restaurants, as they are the only ones who can afford the extortionate rent and rates. This allows councils to focus on shiny new things rather than provide a much-needed lifeline and facilities for the locals. Many small individual businesses have either moved out or simply gone broke. They prefer for you to go out of town to a retail park to do your shopping, at least the parking is generally free. I wonder how much longer before the supermarkets start charging to boost their blotted profits. If you do need to go into your local high street and take the car you will pay ridiculously high parking charges – why? Since Covid parking charges have increased disproportionately to inflation to fleece or deter the motorists. Parking is yet another form of tax. It is viewed as an opportunity for the council to take more of your hard-earned money off you.

All the high streets I have visited throughout the UK are depressing, dirty and in decay. They are simply not nice places anymore. Councils as always do the minimum to maintain their status and make them pleasant, convenient places to visit and shop. Zombie towns are more common than you think, during the day they may be sufferable but at night they are increasingly becoming no go zones to the average local.

Speeding, Road Safety and all that nonsense

To say the road network in the UK is appalling and a disgrace is an understatement. Many roads have more in common with dirt tracks found in third world countries such as India, Africa rather than smooth tarmac roads of a leading nation. Well, if taxing us heavily at the pumps, buying and maintaining car and road/vehicle tax was not enough, then the police and your local council want to bleed the motorist even more in the name of health and safety.

Many Councils and Police forces use the Road Safety and Saving Lives via media and advertising, slogan after slogan in fact it's like spreading jam on toast. They quote statistics that never seem to stack up. However, motoring fines continue to increase year on year. The question to ask is where does the money go? No one knows, one for the treasury to answer, I guess. It certainly is not re-invested back into the roads to try and make them more efficient and user friendly. The roads are so bad; the layout confusing; bus stops are put next to sleeping policemen so vehicles can't pass creating pollution; traffic lights on roundabouts – (why); poorly maintained road marking; potholes galore, all these so-called safety measures create congestion and reduce traffic to a standstill, which equals more pollution. (what will Ed Miliband say?) Then some idiot decided on a 20mph limit creating even more pollution and delay. The answer is simple; they want to make it as complicated (like Tax and the Law) as possible to catch you out and raise money to plug their own financial black hole and bad fiscal management.

I am a cyclist and own three bikes and enjoy getting out and about on the bike, but what idiot dreamt up the new bike law, passing the power of the road to the cyclist? – total moron. The roads are designed for cars and other motor vehicles not pushbikes. If a real person with common sense would have realised that the roads in the UK are that bad, having to keep a metre distance, passing a cyclist is practically impossible and dangerous. Driving down a country lane, you go around a blind corner there is a cyclist the choices are 1. Give the cyclist a metre's distance and swerve into oncoming traffic-death awaits, 2. Slam on the brakes, try not to rear end the cyclist and hope you don't get rear ended by the car coming behind you. What a stupid law! It's the same with potholes, I haven't been on one journey in the last three years when I haven't seen vehicles erratically swerving across the road to avoid a pothole (councils love to avoid paying claims, even though they are liable), many times narrowly missing a car coming the other way. If the council and police were that concerned about safety they would take more care of the road network and fix the millions of potholes. But knowing how the police and councils think rather than fix the potholes they will bring in a stupid law to fine drivers for swerving! Drivers are fed up and frustrated with the constant congestion, so when they get an open road, they simply speed up, surely that's ok right? And there will, of course, be a speed camera waiting for you to take more of your hard-earned cash. The road network in the UK was originally based on getting from A to B as quickly as possible as the rail network started to decay from 1950 onwards. The budget strapped councils and incompetent governments, just keep bleeding the motorist in the UK – the budget strapped councils probably have the mantra - Yes behold the motorist lets bleed them dry.

Travelling across the UK by any vehicle is ridiculously expensive, tiring, with unnecessary long journey times, yes you guessed it, the UK is getting increasingly slower. How slow can we go?

Councils and the highways agency really need a complete overhaul – let's get this country moving.

There are many examples of councils wasting your hard earned money. Council tax only ever goes up and we get more waste bins so we can do their job for them. It's the same people doing an average job at best. It is about time some of these individuals got the sack or had their gold-plated pension schemes stopped. So, keep paying your council tax, just ask yourself what am I paying for? A terrible service is probably your answer!

As with the politicians they should be held to account and they should be sacked and/or have salary clawed back for poor performance. 100's of Millions could be saved with better management. Remember many of these councils/town hall workers do a 30ish hour/4-day week (ever tried calling a council office on a Friday afternoon and ever got a response?). Thought so, incompetent and shambolic, time for change.

Julie Rothchild

Being a politician doesn't mean you are good at anything. That's perhaps except for lying and/or misleading. Do they ever tell the truth?

The Good, the Bad and the Spineless- Pre 2024 Election

As we got close to the 2024 general election the rhetoric, filibustering, bad mouthing and fake promises all followed. In fact, the day Rishi called it, it kicked off. American style audience roadshows, like clowns in a circus talking rubbish and having a hoot. The media love it; the public loathe it. Their behaviour was shambolic, like children in the playground, these are the people that are supposed to set an example for the rest of us to follow. What an example, I ask? No wonder respect in society in general is dwindling. They lack integrity and the willingness to do the right thing that benefits the voter and this country, the narrative only demonstrates their inability to acknowledge the true issues this country faces. The voters watching and listening appeared confused, and the media struggled to provide clarity and make any real sense of what they are saying. Its tiring just watching one of these programmes, an original episode of the 1969 children's program the Clangers makes more sense. I think many of the current political set have been preoccupied by the opening dialogue of the Clangers which talks of a starry blue planet in space and its problems, because they certainly don't focus on the UK and fixing our problems.

Tall stories and fake promises

We all witnessed the political shit show, promise this, promise that time for change – trust us with your way of life, wealth, health and all that stuff. Build the foundations, we won't tax workers or make the economy worse say Labour; bold action, protect the people say the Tories; fairer everything from the Greens; fairer and more fairness from the LibDems and Reform want a contract with you. Yep, the 4-, 6- or 11-point manifesto media sheet got dusted off for us all to see/hear and be amazed at – what hog wash! My biggest issue is that, with the exception of Reform they all must have used the same socialist, left-wing media sheet because they all said the same thing but in different ways. There was nothing to differentiate them, just way left of centre politics. The Tories stopping inheritance tax to win the tory voters back; loudmouth Angela Rayner (Ange) wanting to ban nuclear weapons for the peace vote, millions of houses with no idea of how they will be built, (Ange promised). Yep, the media frenzy ensued, and the voters rolled their eyes once again. The biggest whopper of a promise and an insult to voters is Labour's no tax increases on workers, no one had asked what their definition of a worker was- the press made a blunder there? If Kier pulls it off and there are no tax raises at all (don't worry everyone knows he will raise taxes), then we will be borrowing it and paying it back for decades. The next party in power will inherit the mother of all black holes due to Labour's moment of euphoria, lack of common sense and poor acumen.

How The Parties Shaped Up In England

Over the years there have only been 2 major parties, Conservative (Tories)and Labour, the Liberal Democrats (LibDems) have always been the third party. This election we have a new entrant, Reform the child of UKIP. They won more seats than most expect them to which may add an interesting dynamic as we head for the next general election within 5 years. I covered off the main characters pre-election later. So going into the 2024 election the parties looked like this from my perspective:

Labour was the favourite going into the election, their status gifted by the pathetic squabbling Tories. Whilst the clear favourite, the party did not seem organised, nor does it seem to have answers to the problems the country is facing. It is heavily laden with extremist unions who will apply pressure to Labour to get their way on conditions and pay, and a promise of more strikes to follow, I am sure. I would also expect to see them give councils more opportunity and control to increase council tax with probably no cap or limit. More worrying, they have a big appetite to spend. They will over promise without the funding to support initiatives and are clueless when it comes to implementation, so higher taxes are inevitable and a rapid demise in public service quality will follow. This party did a lot of shouting as the opposition, but it has very few answers. Labour does not make good decisions on their own as they lack experience. What we will see is arrogance and deaf ears to the real problems. They love the freebies, fame and like wasting your hard earned cash.

Reform UK are new and well intentioned, they will receive more votes than people think. Like UKIP, they will appeal to voters who want the best for the UK they are fed up with the Tory Party (who isn't?) and would certainly never vote Labour or LibDem, there are many of these disenfranchised folk out there. For sure, Reform will steal many of the votes and hurt the Tories more than other parties and many Tories will defect on the lead up to, and post-election. Although if they are to make the gains, they predict they will have to get a move on and establish a presence in every constituency and gain a few more political celebrities to support their cause. Nigel Farage and Suella Braverman joining forces could be a game changer if it happens. Reform do appear to have more pragmatism and common sense than any other party and speak the language of normal people suffering the daily challenges of UK society. Many say they are far right wing, I say given the immigration nightmare we are facing they're nearer the middle ground than you think – more traditional Tory, more work to do Reform.

The Tories are pretty much finished this time round and will need to do something extraordinary to make something half decent of the result that is coming their way. The whole party and the Whitehall brigade fuelling the chaos only have themselves to blame, what a mess they have made~. First David Cameron after a landslide victory acts like a petulant child and hands his notice in after he got Brexit wrong, he clearly failed to read the mood of the country. Then we had Teresa May (why) then Boris who got stabbed in the back by his own team over party gate, followed by Liz Truss with bad financial for thought and timing issue, again stabbed in the back. Now we have Rishi, enough said. This party is arrogant, hanging their dirty washing out for all to see, rather than working as a team and delivering for the very voters who put them in power. Despite their failings they are probably the only party that has the experience and tool kit collectively at this stage to run the country for the better-though squabbling children spring to mind.

The LibDems claim to fame was in May 2010 when the coalition government was created with the conservative party to keep Labour out of power; it lasted until 2016 (Wikipedia). The LibDems are an interesting crowd and have never really amounted to much. I do not see that changing for the next election either or the one thereafter. They kind of sit in the middle of everything and achieve nothing. They appear to be strong in privileged woke areas where the voters want nothing to change – 'We are the comfortable crowd; everything here is fine'. The UK we live in today really does need to change and fast, the majority of the country want change for the better that's why many will vote Labour or Reform over Conservative, but not LibDem as they would spend more time talking, employing consultants to tell them the answer before making a decision. My personal experience with them demonstrates this, I challenged a local Councillor who said he would answer any question I had, so I asked why the local council has removed the recycling of glass from the local tip (this is a local annoying issue), when it is one of the most recyclable materials known to man. His reply was 'that's a tricky one, its complicated, we can't really influence that issue, there are contract issues' and promptly made his excuses and left my doorstep. I rest my case. Strong LibDem areas will always be strong as they are normally wealthy and left wing – the 'do nothing party'.

What a bunch to choose from

I viewed the current candidates pre 2024 election with a simple rule of thumb (as with all elections) the '**good**' are strong leaders, honest, straight talkers – tell it how it really is, wanting the best for the voting people of the UK and putting them first. They challenge the status quo, act responsibly and set a good example. That's what I want to vote for. Clearly that's a rare thing in this day and age. Perhaps the definition of a politician should be changed to a word that reflects what we must suffer from them today – a mountebank or a charlatan. The '**bad**' rating is the opposite to good, and then there is the '**spineless**' which is bad with extra pitiful traits, like constantly making bad decision/U-turns; being a puppet for the left; lacking any form of passion. The worst trait being too scared to look in the mirror, blaming everybody around them for their poor decision making, the Teflon effect – nothing will ever stick, or so they think. That's why we need the free press. So, using my optic, let's have a look at the political movers, shakers and players around 2023-24 as we go into the election around Apr-May 2024.

Kier Starmer

I am sure that Sir Kier was well deserving of the knighthood he received in 2014 as head of the Crown Prosecution Service (CPS). Although from what I read, a knighthood is given as a tradition to those who head the very controversial and heavily criticised department. Therefore, it's not based upon on whether they did a good job or not, they get the title regardless, it would appear. Perhaps that's why he doesn't like being called 'Sir', maybe he feels in the back of his mind that he is not deserving of the title? I have a better title for Kier, but that will come later. Many of his speeches and interviews that I watch, he seems torn, awkward, at odds with himself pre-election. It's the way he delivers a speech, with a lack of passion and conviction, as though he was just reading from someone else's script. He certainly does not convince me he is a leader, an individual I can trust, or that he can deliver on a promise. This becomes evident very quickly if his bum is in the seat at No 10, U-turn after U-turn and broken promises galore. His choice of deputy also needs to be challenged. Loudmouth Angela does neither him nor the party any favours in terms of image. She is obviously popular among the unions given the level of donations she receives, but I am not sure the public are fond of her. Kier's support for the unions sounds a desperate cry for help and support, the wrong kind of help and support in my mind if you are the leader of a party. He will ultimately become the puppet for the left-wing elite and the socialist unions. I challenge you to catch a train these days that is running on time or running at all. The unions' desire to drag the country further into the gutter is alarming. Keir will be unable to stop them. He is more like a Liberal Democrat, unsure what to say or do, lacking strong leadership. Although he seems relatively resilient as his credentials suggest, taking on challenges, for example the Steven Lawance case, navigating a political and controversial hot potato whilst at the CPS. This just keeps him out of the spineless ranking for now, but firmly in the **Bad** camp.

Rachel Reeves

Most politicians who get a senior job in the cabinet, are usually unqualified for it or have little experience. Rachel is one of these, having a degree, working at the bank of England and chairing the Business, Energy and Industrial Strategy Committee (we all know how successful that was as we experience the impact on energy prices). These credentials do not make you a good chancellor. Apparently, she is competent with numbers like most people who can work out a basic profit and loss account (P&L

for the technical folk). These are the fundamental challenges of managing a bank account and staying in the black (in credit), rather than going overdrawn, owing the bank, and being in the red. For any chancellor the world over it has more zeros on the numbers than your average public bank account. I suspect Rach, will start with," I have been left with only a bean in the bank, and I will have to make (wait for it) some difficult and/ or tough decisions because I need at least 3 beans in the bank." Blame the Tories as the Tories blamed Gordon Brown and dodgy Tony, so she will use the classic Chancellor playbook. Like most chancellors over the last thirty years, I have never seen a Chancellor embrace the challenge with a positive perspective and offer solutions and real opportunities to generate wealth. It shows their inexperience, lack of understanding of how businesses work and a lack of good acumen. The usual phrases will be rolled out at every opportunity i.e. 'Those with the broadest shoulders will be at the sharp end of the budget', This translates to - under Labour those of you who work the hardest, take the risks, save their cash, look after their investment and are careful with your money, will pay the most tax, so the lazy don't have to get off their backsides and get a job. It's a clear **spineless** rating.

Angela Rainer

So, the 'wanna, wanna be leader, sorry deputy', certainly is no Spice Girl by ambition, or someone who wants to work hard to be successful, unlike Baby, Sporty, Ginger, Posh and Scary. She is probably the worst role model politician I have seen in recent times. I truly respect that she came from the working class and was bought up in poverty. It is tough, join the club luv-like many, many others. However, the bar she has set to demonstrate success is appallingly low. To give Ange the benefit of the doubt, her predecessors and role models in the Labour party have not exactly been great, very far from it, so what has she really aspired to be. Ange presents herself as a working-class lass and wants the best for the people (what people, please be specific), however that's where she might have started, but Ange is a chancer and has nothing from what I see to back up any of her arguments. She likes to blur the lines of accountability as all extreme-left wingers do; it's always someone else's fault. Try getting a straight answer. Ange lacks substance detail and is so unconvincing when she faces challenges and questions from others, she appears out of her depth but loves the camera, limelight and attention it brings over doing her real job for those people she harps on about. Given the levels of union and socialist donations she raises, beware Kier, a dark challenger is coming when the knives come out. I am sure she means well and wants to eradicate the poverty and strife that she suffered in Stockport during the eighties. However, I have no sympathy. Poverty and strife are worse now in the UK than it has ever been and building more new homes will not solve the problem. So, Ange playing the poor old me card, 'I struggled poor old me.' is just a fake headline. For me she has forgotten her roots and is focussed on a better life, not for the many but a better life for number 1. Ange is clearly in the **Bad** camp.

Rishi Sunak

As the outgoing PM and leader of the Conservative party (the writing is on the wall), it's been an interesting journey of skullduggery, internal rivalry, and self-interest of all those involved in school playground antics. Doing your dirty washing in public simply switched off the voters in their droves. The saying goes, 'If you can't sort your own house out, how could you possibly sort out and run the country?'

Rishi seems like a nice guy working hard and trying his best, but he is lacking core elements in his life skills toolbox, i.e. strong leadership, (trying to please all the people all of the time), and good decision and policy making. Bringing back Dave Cameron was a big mistake, what really drove him to make that decision is beyond me. Dave had one big election success as Conservative leader, but then he put all his eggs in one basket and punted for Remain. Dave really failed to acknowledge the oppositions' argument or the mood of the country. He showed outright arrogance, like so many politicians, and bet his job on it. His career then went to the dogs. Andrew Pierce of the Daily Mail 14/11/23, branded Dave Cameron as 'completely gutless' and I must agree. Gutless Dave is clearly at odds with the country when it comes to Europe. His key agenda will be to get us back in bed with his buddies in the unelected European parliament, not to worry, I don't think they are going to win.

Then Rishi made another bad decision to exit Priti Patel who was starting to take the issue of immigration and law and order head on, a totally committed and focussed individual, ticking a lot of good politician boxes in my mind. Yep, another bad move by Rishi. However, his biggest mistake, which sums up how stupid and left wing the party has become in the last decade, was doing the dirty on Suella Braverman (more on her later), Suella, like Priti, started to show real leadership and accountability – straight talking, strength of character. It was too much for Rishi, he gave a weak excuse for both their departures. I suspect the real reason was they were becoming too popular and patriotic for his liking. Rishi probably got noised up as the two ladies stepped on the toes of senior civil servants which they don't like. I can imagine the pair complaining about how lazy civil servants are and them telling the civil servants to get on with their day jobs, do it properly, and work a full week like most tax paying citizens. So rather than enhance Suella and Priti's skills, building strength and sorting out the many problems the country has, Rishi saw it as a threat and wielded the axe.

Rishi is an unelected PM, but secured the party vote, after the obvious witch hunt that led to Boris standing down and the disaster that followed with lettuce Lizz Truss' poorly thought through attempt at being PM. Genuinely I think her strategy had legs, but she went too quickly and spooked the city. Rishi was gifted a golden opportunity to turn the party around, lead from the front and re-unite it and kill off the internal bickering. However, rather than lead he took out the strong politicians that could have helped him address the weakness of the party. Further mistakes then followed, and the party simply imploded. The lack of leadership has led to further infighting and divide for the whole country to witness via the media.

Rishi and his side kick Mr Hunt talk about those difficult and tough decisions but haven't made any since being in power. From what I can see, they are just rolling out the same old scripts time and time again. He really likes the easy life, avoids confrontation at all costs and hopes that the noise will fade away. It's the **spineless** rating for Rishi.

Humza Yousaf

Humza is not unlike big mouth Ange, in that he seems to speak before he engages his brain. Since he became the leader of the SNP, he has shown a complete lack of leadership and bad decision making. He had a great opportunity after Nicola Sturgeon left. He couldn't do much worse right? Wrong the SNP popularity has fallen off a cliff, membership of the party is at an all-time low, all as a direct consequence of his poor leadership. In some ways he is like Sadiq Khan in that he looks to deflect everything and blame anyone other than himself for the mess he has created. His leadership will be short lived after the next election. Humza is **spineless** and was never going to cut it. A vote of no confidence sealed the deal to exit the very left-wing politician. The SNP electing the new leader John Swinney the second time around is an interesting play, but I think he is too liberal and will end up doing nothing as a leader. Time will tell.

Suella Braverman

Suella stands out as a strong leader and visionary, predicting the outcomes of mass illegal migration and the persecution of white males in the UK which is so blatant to see from the far left and Woke mob. Suella reads the room, analyses the mass of data available to her, and outlines what is going to happen in the next 5-10 years in the UK. She is a bright and attentive politician; her constituents have many positive things to say about her. She does not appear to shy away from challenging topics (which she demonstrated as Home Secretary) and representing the views of the majority, challenging the status quo, not afraid to tell the truth and more importantly did not apologise for telling it – great work. Suella is straight talking and it would appear that she does not suffer fools gladly, a similar welcome style to the way Nigel Farage goes about business. Recently she defended the white male contingent of the country, it's about time someone had the honesty to do so. Apparently, they have rights too. Suella, also spoke out about the misguided dogma of multiculturalism in The Times (27/9/23) which sums up some of the real challenges - one for Kier to opine. Whilst it is blatantly obvious to most people in the street, she seems to have thoroughly worked out how the privileged lefties and woke poison are damaging the country.

Suella is one of the most refreshing politicians of our time and speaks the truth. Many suggest that she is a scaremonger on the immigration issues facing the UK. I would say if her statement were not true, go and visit places in the UK, cities such as Nottingham, Bristol, Birmingham, Leicester or Boston in Lincolnshire, Slough, Peterborough and East London as a starter and tell me that immigration is not changing the face and culture of the UK. Suella has both the vision and the resolve to take the challenges head on and does not want to please everyone all the time. After all that's the job of a politician, do what the voters, who voted you in want. Sorry, Guardian readers and wokealites - it's called doing what's right for the majority not the minority.

Rishi would have had a stronger position before and after the 2024 elections if he had respected and acknowledged her skill set, rather than listening to the shadows of Westminster and sticking the knife in. Suella would be a great asset to any party; her political stance is perhaps more aligned with Reform at present, than the current Conservative mantra which is leaning more socialist left. I could see her being PM one day when politicians realise the country is so fed up with weak and poor decision making and spineless politicians. Suella gets a **good** rating.

Nigel Farage

Nigel is a charismatic individual, loathe him, or like him he has done more than any other politician in recent decades to shake the tree and stimulate the political debate encouraging people to talk about politics. This man gave the UK hope and along with Boris, got the leave (EU) vote done. He has common sense, resolve and is happy to take on anything and give a common-sense real person's perspective rather than the elite's no answer. If he does not know the answer, he will take it away rather than bluster his way through and lie. Nigel will ask difficult questions and challenge the status quo, much to the disgust of presenters; liberals; wokesters and of course other politicians. The truth hurts, but that's what we need more of in politics - Truth.

Like Matt Hancock the ex-Health Secretary who did time in the jungle in 2022, Nigel followed suit in 2023. He was very popular and did his image many favours. I think he spoke a lot of sense, not only did he give his view, but he had also the rare ability as a politician to listen to others and respond to the question rather than avoid it and prattle on. We saw the real man, who does not suffer fools gladly in a face-to-face environment, in fact very close proximity. He is confident in his own ability and leadership style which comes across well. It certainly upped his rating, as does his role as presenter of GB News. He highlights and covers difficult topics with honesty, calling for action to be taken against the incompetent behaviour of the government, the opposition and the silly far left stupidity, we all witness on a day-to-day basis. Unlike most political folk Nigel offers perspective and solutions to problems, rather than just ranting or deflecting. GB News, where he presents, it's very current and very now. I, like many of you are pleased that he has returned to mainstream politics to keep the many bad and spineless individuals on their toes. If Nigel and Suella joined forces the Reform party would be unstoppable, Labour and the Conservatives would have a real challenge on their hands in the next election. Nigel easily gets a **good** rating; he wants real change and better outcomes for UK and its citizens.

Ed Davey

Sir Ed seems a nice, jolly individual and well meaning. He received his knighthood in 2016 for political and public service. As Postal affairs minister 2010-12, it is quite frankly embarrassing that he refuses to give back his knighthood for his role in the disgraceful saga under his watch. Another demonstration of weakness and lack of accountability from a politician pointing the finger at everyone else other than himself. This is a trait of mediocrity which sums up the LibDems' stance and view of the country. Suggesting he was misled is a joke; it seems to me that he didn't really know the right questions to ask in the board room, subsequently showing a firm lack of experience to do the job. He was reported on The Independent online (25/2/2024) as saying he should have apologised for the post office mess earlier. The problem is he didn't, he was too frightened to speak up or apply common sense to what was being presented to him at the board. He just hoped it would go away. There is no doubt that the scandal will hurt the number of votes the Liberal Democrats receive. I think he is likely to step down after the next general election or maybe before, after he gives evidence at the Post Office Horizon inquiry. The minutes of the Board would make an interesting read. The post office saga will continue to haunt him, putting him in a difficult place. As leader he has too much baggage. Ed easily fits the **bad** category.

Sadiq Khan

This individual is a political agitator and most certainly a hypocrite. I think if there was ever a poll outside of London for the most unpopular mayor, he would win outright. The best example of his hypocrisy is the Congestion Charge lie he throws around, ULEZ introduced in 2019, Sadiq says, it's about improving air quality for Londoners, because the combustion engine was killing families and their children or so the data says. Does anyone trust his data? Ok that's great and very moral - I agree. However, Sadiq then says if you pay me a fee of 10-£15 per day you can come and pollute London as much as you want to. If the pollution is that bad, then stop it all together, but no. I question his reasoning. Sadiq has been unable to manage his budget estimated around £15billion, there is a massive shortfall. He is desperate, so yet again he wants the taxpayer to pay increasingly more money to solve his incompetent budgeting and poor decision making rather than improve the air quality for his Londoners and millions of visitors to the capital. Sadiq's strategy is a contradiction and regressive, he is quick to take the money but very slow to invest in a cleaner environment and policies to help Londoners go greener. Furthermore, if he cared about the people of London why has he not addressed the pollution and shocking filth of the tube, rather than spend £6m on renaming tube stations with new signage in an attempt to win the woke minority vote as reported in the Daily Mail (16th Feb 2024). Also, more importantly he should address knife crime and the death of young adults/children which under his watch has got seismically worse according to the Office of National Statistics and every other data source. More people have died from knife crime and indeed terror attacks than from pollution, from what I can see. It's difficult to comprehend what he really stands for. It appears to me that it's all about him and no one else, he certainly likes spending taxpayers' money on promoting his re-election 2024 message. Maybe I am not looking hard enough however, it's difficult to find much positive content or likeable attributes about him. As a regular reader of the London Metro and Evening Standard, it appears many of the readers are extremely frustrated with the mayor's performance. Although, his own mayor of London and TFL websites do put a very positive spin on him, Sadiq appears Anti British and certainly not patriotic, far from it. This is a man who bans taxi drivers from putting Union Jacks on their vehicles to celebrate the Euros and doesn't like the advertising of hot dogs, or as the Americans say wieners, on the tube. However, he is more than happy to have Palestinian flags flying in the streets of East London and allow a controversial Islamic preacher to advertise on his transport network across London.

Too much self-promotion and 'look at me' does tend to harbour insecurity in an individual Sadiq. Calling the Tories morally rotten regarding the handling of the Richard Tice saga for calling Sadiq a 'lying, corrupt racist' (GBNews 23/8/23) is laughable and is another display of an individual who needs to take a good look in the mirror. Sadiq like Ed Davey points the finger and blames everyone else, rather than address his own failings. In my ranking there is no hesitation giving this mayor an outright **spineless** rating, and Trump for what it is worth agrees.

The Sun (24th June 1998) ran the headline and ask the question 'Is Tony Blair the most dangerous man in Britian?'. For me yes, he was then, and he still is in the top five now. However, since then he has had a few challengers to that title in my mind, namely Kier and Corbyn, but firmly in the lead is Sadiq, surely, he must be on the MI5/MI6 watch list?

Jeremy Hunt

It's a bit unfortunate having a surname that people play on when it's not going well and compare you to a certain part of a woman's anatomy. That aside he seems happy and always excited when he has an interview. He hasn't been in the chancellor's seat very long and he did inherit a bit of a mess from Liz and Quashi, but in his short stint the economy is starting to trend upwards. His calm influence means the City have warmed to him. He always seems to talk sense and have credible information to support his point. I don't feel that as a chancellor he wants to borrow my watch and charge me to tell me the time. He has just got on with the job he was paid to do. He edges into a **good** rating.

When politicians deliberately ignore the writing on the wall and choose not to act and do the right thing, it shows their contempt for the very people they are supposed to represent and protect.

Julie Rothchild

Immigration – National Self Harm

Every Government of the last 30 years in the UK is embarrassed by the immigration and asylum-seeker topic and so they should be. What a complete mess – who is to blame for it? Many years have passed, and Governments have come and gone, having done little, virtually nothing to address the issue and bring it under control; in contrast to countries such as Hungary, Australia and Israel. Legal immigration is acceptable when it is, for a purpose, controlled and a benefit to a nation. However, in the UK, mass immigration is like a critical medical condition namely cancer- insidious, silently spreading, painful on many levels and often hidden from sight by the government. If you don't address it in the early stages and take drastic action, it accelerates fast and the inevitable happens. In this case, total meltdown in the form of significant economic burden; Public Service failure; Infrastructure crumbles; widespread unrest, chaos and cultural erosion quickly follow (tell me if the afore mentioned points do not describe the UK - the takeover is in full swing). Immigration is doing exactly that and as of 2025 under Labour, there is and will continue to be a significant increase- it's out of control, the figures do not lie. Look through your own moral lens at the UK with an open mind at what is happening in front of your eyes it's not even a bad joke; it's an horrific mess and there is worse to come. Before you read on, let me clarify what I mean by the phrase 'illegals'. These are not people who have been displaced or irregular. No, they are individuals who come to the UK shore/

airport deliberately without the correct travel documentation to confirm their identity, their background and values, or indeed the country from which they originated (in some cases) – This is unlawful in the UK, so let's call it what it is 'illegal'.

The Government and civil servants adopt a very divisive tactic, keep quiet, tell half a story and the problem will go away (haven't we heard that one before!) The illegals are given hotels, three meals a day and access to many exclusive perks and benefits, which most working-class folk, single parent families and pensioners could only dream about. The illegals are then dispersed by stealth into local communities, towns and cities without the consent or even knowledge of the voting public, (sometimes local councils) hoping no one will notice. 20-30 years ago, this was not a problem, their numbers were small. Now there are so many and the numbers so high it's like a bomb going off as 500-1000 at a time turn up and take over an all-inclusive hotel. The impact on the everyday voting person in the street is ignored behind this political embarrassment and shambolic management of immigration. It smacks of an inability to think the issues through and have a clear strategy that focuses and favours the UK and its people, not the European Parliament or International Law. Whilst we see lies, cover ups, half-truths on many fronts, this is the most dishonest picture painted by the governments over the last 20 years of the so-called benefits of immigration and more recently the real issues associated with mass illegal immigration. There is growing public anger, media uproar/disbelief and an unprecedented level of incompetence from the border force, immigration service and government – will someone in Westminster just do their job and sort it out? We all knew the immigration situation was bad, now we have more (not enough) facts/ figures about the individuals who arrive on our shores illegally and it's worse than we thought. Clearly, they are here for the freebies the government dishes out with no strings attached.

Immigration agenda heats up

Being a small Island the immigration topic has been bubbling along for the last 25-30 years in this country. In 1997 - 2007 we had good old Tony Blair and his merry men promoting the UK as a place to come and prosper, a bit like the American dream but without the dream. Everything is free and of course vote Labour when you get here to keep the Tories out. It's difficult to disagree with Sally-Ann Hart (GB News Sept 2024) who suggests that dodgy Tony went out of his way to change the face of the UK without seeking the consent of the British public. In my opinion, Labour under Kier, will continue to ignore its own citizens in the same way Tony did, in favour of immigrants from other countries, Somewhere, where Islamist extremism is the norm. I remember in the late nineties how disgusted my friends were, saying Labour reps had been handing leaflets out to the poor across some African states and Europe. These leaflets promoted the welfare system and the support that immigrants would receive upon entering the UK. These included big opportunities and no surprise, welcomed them to Labour's view of the world. After the long labour stint of Blair and Brown being in power, the voting people of the UK became fed up with the lack of control of our borders and the increasing numbers of the wrong type of immigrants - 'The Illegals'. The sacrifice and disruption to the British way of life and all that it stood for, started then. There is no doubt that controlled immigration after the second world war helped to rebuild this country and helped the UK prosper, hence these people should be treated equally as UK citizens. They contributed considerably and should therefore share in the prosperity that ensued. Society has moved on significantly since the war; on the flip side, it's a disaster that politicians and the laws haven't – the politicians just keep blaming each other like school children.

However, Blair got carried away. He sent off British service personnel to fight a war in Afghanistan that was built upon blatant lies about weapons of mass destruction. His public sector bills soared out of control burning taxpayers' cash and sunk the UK into massive debt. Many voters were so disenchanted that they swapped from Labour back to the Conservatives in protest. Meanwhile Nigel Farage started to form his ideas for the UKIP party, clearly seeing an opportunity in mainstream politics and the blur it was becoming with its lack of priority for the UK citizens. The hot air and fake promises to control migration were so obvious that the UKIP party started to gain votes and became a major player in politics. UKIP's overall mantra was to look after the people of the UK and address the voters' concerns. Yes, UKIP ignored the so-called polls and focused on talking to the public and listening, rather than relying on the polls that are so frequently dressed up as fact. UKIP's USP was Illegal Immigration and the outright contempt for the unelected EU parliament and its stupid rules. The other parties just continued the same old stories with a lack of substance, trying to be on the EU/international stage like celebrities hungry for fame. In 2016 even Nigel and the Brexit party were a big influence in the referendum for leaving the EU rather than remaining. Boris saw the opportunity to build upon the story, add a few twists and extra (fake) promises and the vote was set. Yes, we left the EU, but did we? Even Nigel thought the Remain vote would edge it (I 24/6/2016) but it was a close vote.

Whilst the main parties claim that immigration is not the top of voters' list of concerns, because they had been led by their noses by the polls- it's the NHS, it's the economy, its fuel, poverty etc. I beg to differ. A large proportion of the UK's voting citizens is strongly against both legal and illegal immigration and wants much stricter control of the UK borders and robust pro-UK process for allowing any form of immigration. A very worried and confused incumbent at number 10 Downing Street, Dave Cameron, decided to play chicken with the British voting public in 2016 and the European referendum was announced. The popularity of Nigel and Boris Johnson in the Leave camp became increasingly stronger and surprised everyone. Whether you are a Leaver, or a Remainer (Remoaner), democracy had spoken, and the majority voted to leave the EU. However, is this really the case? Politics being politics, it was painfully slow, they love red tape, posh dinners and not committing to anything. It finally happened at 11pm on 31st January 2020. Did it really need to take that long? I wonder how many government specialists and consultants we really needed and at what cost to the UK taxpayer – not value for money in my opinion.

The media have played down the immigration card as not being the number one reason we left the EU, citing many different reasons, even though not one day goes by without small boats being reported in the newspapers or on TV: or the unbelievable shocking numbers of the legal immigration being waved though the system. In 2024 the home office issued around 1.4million visas. Suella Braverman described it as a 'national disaster' (Daily Mail 1/3/24), I couldn't agree more. Immigration was the biggest problem 30 years ago and it remains so today (2025). In my opinion and that of everyone I have spoken to in the last 10 years on this topic, illegal immigration is the number one issue. It's out of control and that's why the country is in such a mess. Just look at the faces and body language of any PM talking on the issue or attending (another talking shop) summit and the look of desperation is there to be witnessed.

Illegals Get a Priority Pass

The cost of immigration varies depending on who you ask or what you read but the current financial measurement is only one side of the story. You are told a number and expected to believe it. If the Government tell you a figure, it's normally the lowest, as they constantly try to make good of a very embarrassing situation. Current estimate (2023) suggests that it's on average £17-18m a day. My view is, double it (based upon the overrun of central and local Government estimated spend and projects such as HS2. That began at £30bn, then increased to £56bn, then £150bn and it's still rising. So, the real cost is probably £36m a day and increases rapidly daily. As a line in the sand, it's between £7bn-£14bn in 2023/24, excluding the cost of hotels. But I also think that is erring on the side of modesty. The above numbers probably account for billed receipts directly attributed to immigration not the additional indirect services such as the navy, lifeboat, fire brigade, doctors, nurses and ambulance services etc., re-directed from their day jobs, which is looking after and protecting the UK citizens, but instead its prioritising the illegals. That's to redirected resources and services you as a taxpayer should be benefiting from. It's not just costs at the end of the day. More importantly it's the negative impact on people's health, those on the NHS waiting lists – the ever-growing queue of people with a promise of treatment who are then de-prioritised consequently remaining on waiting lists longer and longer. In the meantime, 'fresh off the boat illegals' get treated. Let's not forget who gets priority on housing. They get a GP appointment on demand while you do the e-consult. I have not seen my doctor face to face for 5 years, instead I have received diagnoses via text. Does this sound familiar? Consider the indirect numbers and unbilled receipts and they probably double again. So, the true cost is probably nearer £70 - 100bn a year. Will they ever tell us the true numbers or simply keep fudging them to cover their embarrassment? Whatever the number it's putting a massive hole in our economy, a lot more than the alleged £20bn that Rachel in accounts keeps harping on about. When it comes to telling the truth about money the Politicians and Senior Civil Servants continue to dance around their handbags, like inadequate, awkward teenagers at their first school disco! How about giving an all-inclusive hotel priority pass to some of the UK's homeless veterans and children on our streets? That would be money well spent.

So why are so many people fed up with the Illegals?

The media try to do a good job exposing what's happening on our shores and in our airspace, but they never seem to recount it or view it from the public perspective; the suffering of day-to-day issues created by illegal immigration. We can all see that the majority of illegals are young, war age men, who say they are here to be free and live a safe happy family life. I believe an extremely small number are genuine, maybe 1%. Those are the ones who travel with their families when they cross the channel. Not young men wearing designer sports gear – Adidas trainers, Nike tops and joggers, brandishing a new shiny mobile phone. Nor the ones that arrive on our shores tooled up with knives and other weapons – if the UK is the safe place, why bring a weapon? It is clear to me that most illegals are here for free handouts, great benefits or crime related activities. It's nothing to do with freedom/being safe, it's the free stuff, I can do what I want, and I don't have to work for it and when I bring my family, they get the same privileges.

Also, one must ask oneself, what type of individual leaves their family behind? The young war age men that come here seem very able and athletic. Jumping on and off a dingy in the water, it's like watching 'Total Wipeout' or 'It's a Knockout'. Should they not be at home looking after their family fighting for their freedom rather than abandoning them and leaving the women and children to suffer in apparently terrible conditions and do the fighting? They certainly look fit enough to work. But, yet again the authorities and local councils fail to challenge them and just give in. Apparently in the UK you must believe everything these people tell you and despite not one of them contributing anything to our society, they get everything. Do we really want this type of individual in our society? They appear to be of no use in their own country so what use are they going to be here?

Many elderly people and families struggle in the UK to heat their homes in the winter and feed themselves, sometimes it's a case of one or the other. Eat and go cold or be warm and starve.

So apparently, we are not quite a third world country? Many of these people have worked all their lives, paid their taxes, saved for a rainy day and followed the rules as recommended by the governments of the day. Yet they still get fleeced by corporate UK with extortionate prices for food, fuel and heating. However, if you're fresh off the boat or lorry- a freeloader- then you'll be provided with a warm hotel room, three meals a day, a translator and free legal support if you want to complain about anything. The UK systems, policy and law are totally inadequate to manage the issue we are faced with. To make it worse, they seem to get priority over your child in education, childcare and housing depending on what council area they end up in. The illegals get all this free stuff without question.

In the meantime, the British workers who are being relentlessly screwed by the government with ever increasing taxes, struggling to make ends meet and go about their day - these are the same people paying for the immigration freebies. The moral playing field in this scenario is neither equal nor fair and the government knows it but refuses to give comment to it. However, the public's frustration and growing anger will continue as will the protests outside the all-inclusive hotels where these people live. Why shouldn't the peaceful protests be aimed at the government and authorities? Who got us signed up for the European Human Rights Act? Who set the immigration policy? Who controls law & order? And who runs/owns our boarders? They come because the UK is too soft and gullible, and we don't want to upset the do-gooders and lefties, do we?

Is anyone asking the right questions about Immigration?

Who is asking the right questions? Well, with all the quangos and overpaid civil servants, government consultants, the statistics and information on the immigration hurricane hitting the UK, the questions should be obvious. The real challenge is whether anyone is asking the right questions and drawing the right conclusions – the simple answer is no. In addition, the media always tends to focus on the soft emotional issue when speaking to illegals just in case they might offend or upset them.

In order for me to grasp the real impact of illegals, it would be helpful to know from the government; what are the real numbers coming to our shores and what is the true cost to the taxpayer (more on that later). Also, how many have criminal records; what is their overall contribution to the overall rising crime rates in the UK (we have only just got this); how many just disappear from the hotels/centres and are unaccounted for; how many are of a workable age and how many are working and paying in; demographics split between gender/age. Whilst some of these numbers are reported and talked about none of them are ever the true numbers. The government needs to stop hiding from immigration and sort it out, please stop fudging the numbers to cover your embarrassment.

From a mainstream media perspective, (in particular channel 4, Sky and the BBC) they need to stop sitting on their hands and start obtaining some real answers from the illegals and the government – stop towing the line and giving the PC dialogue. We need more honesty and challenge like GB news. How about some informative questions to the government? For example why do illegals get priority over UK nationals on housing, healthcare, benefits, schooling; why have the immigration laws not been strengthened to return the illegals back to their first place of entry into Europe (other countries have done it); why are we putting illegals in hotels with three meals a day, when pensioners and some families in the UK struggle so much. The killer question to the current labour government should be why do you clearly favour illegals over your own nationals– while this once great country loses its identity, culture and history? The problem is when you call out the politicians on this subject, they really cannot explain themselves, so they rely on well-worn cliches such as "It's a complex issue" or "It's more difficult than you think" – what utter nonsense!

Laughable Stories – Gullible State – No Common Sense

So, we have established that the immigration service, border control government are clearly not doing their job of protecting our borders and consequently are putting the public at risk on many fronts. The media have reported a number of stories, which tell of the woes of these immigrants (mainly young war age men) which makes me laugh in disbelief about how gullible the authorities and media are to the stories of woe. Common sense and objectivity have gone out of the window. The media regularly points out these, quite frankly stupid cases, in an attempt to tell the public how bad things really are and how the people in authority are both weak and incompetent. How can many of these cases even reach court and be heard? There is a clue somewhere here (wakey wakey, sleepy government) in these stories of woe. The law needs to be fundamentally overhauled. That does not mean tweaking it around the edges in a false attempt to hide embarrassment and give the impression you are taking it seriously.

ITV news (22/1/24 news at 10pm) showed a group of illegal young men, apparently, they claimed to be children under the age of 18 years. There was a suggestion that these young men were at risk to child abuse because they had to share accommodation with older men in hotels in the UK. Two men to a room. One individual said that he had to share a room with an older Arab man, and he was frightened, he spoke a different language, and he could not understand him - welcome to our world! The majority of the telephone customer service we receive in the UK are from companies such as TalkTalk, Virgin, Amazon, Dell etc. who outsourced their customer service operations abroad. Equally, some of the NHS workers, my family, friends and I have experienced conversations with people who cannot speak or understand English – it's absolutely disgraceful that they have a job and cannot converse adequately in English, but I am not scared or frightened. It's also hilarious that he managed to sleep rough, congregate and travel across Europe and board a boat with all sorts of different nationalities who also don't speak the same language, but apparently now he is in the UK he is upset and scared – really! How gullible have the authorities and the media become – pathetic! Rather than believe the story of woe and utter rubbish, why is the interviewer not asking real questions such as, If you are apparently only 15 years old how did you afford the £10k fee to the smuggler who got you here? Where is your ID to confirm your age? You managed to bring your phone and have a picture on it, yet you left all other forms of ID – how spurious! How did you afford all the designer gear you are wearing? When can we check your dental records/teeth to establish your true age? When you came across the channel did you carry a weapon for protection? If you have nothing to hide and you are here for genuine reasons those should be simple questions to answer. The truth is that the majority of illegals are lying and are here for very different reasons than what they claim to be.

How about the polish drug dealer Nikodem Lopata, who claims he does not speak Polish, so he is able to avoid deportation (Telegraph 28/2/2025). How about a tough stand, learn it when you go back. It's shameful that some idiot accepts this excuse and lets him off. The reason he doesn't want to return is because he will feel the full brunt of the Polish people and their legal system, neither of which are very accepting of drug dealers, unlike the UK. I suspect he has been coached to say the right things to avoid deportation. But the judge could not see common sense.

And then we have all seen the online (where was the censorship?) bragging of illegals in hotel rooms with their all-inclusive perks, the one that probably summed up the gloating attitude of the war age men was in the Sun (The Sun 4/4/25) when they exposed two men boasting of the perks and their hotel room, whilst in stark contrast, UK families struggle.

You have the AK47 gun maniac Isak Bruna, who fled Albania for the UK to escape prosecution and imprisonment in 2013. Apparently due to a loophole he cannot be deported. Probably the same loophole used by the convicted serial rapist Mohammed Aslam. It took over 26 years to try and deport him, but apparently, he has been here too long and established a life in the UK, according to the Sun (4/8/24). I read these articles in total disbelief – how stupid and gullible is the law to those fake stories from criminals.

Well, it's not just a UK problem. The majority of Europe are fed up too. We are seeing in 2023-25 a massive swing to parties of the right. People feel ignored and taken advantage of. The left and moderate governments have ignored the warning signs over the years. Like the proverbial ostrich, they seem to bury their heads in the sand and just hope the problem goes away, but it is getting worse, and the voters simply swerve back to the right. A typical example is the Dutch election and the rise of Geert Wilders and France with Marine Le Pen. More European countries will follow, as will the UK in the next general election. Time is up lefties; you had your chance and failed.

Impact of Immigration

The impact is easy to see, not only is it a matter of cost and cultural erosion, but the infrastructure in the UK cannot cope with the folk who leave here as legal citizens. To put it in perspective, the illegals' number alone (60-90k a year) is the size of a large town or small city. When did we last build a new town or city? Not recently, just ugly housing estates with no facilities or infrastructure to support the needs of the homeowners adequately. Or is that the new integration experiment? Persuade taxpayers to buy these ugly carboard houses, then move in illegals next door who have paid nothing, and it will work out fine - heard that somewhere before. It's no wonder we have a housing crisis driven by both forms of immigration. The simple answer is, no immigration no housing crisis. The number of illegals and legals is dragging the UK to that third world status quicker than ever - sucking the UK dry, like locusts attacking farmland.

There are many articles of people living in areas where the illegals have been shipped in, in bulk. House prices plummet, crime increases, and public services deteriorate. The public are becoming more frightened and threatened, it's no surprise as these individuals have no identity, known history. They could be murderers, rapists, drug dealers and/or extremists. Perhaps the public should run their own experiment? Let's move every UK serving politician/senior civil servant next door to a group of immigrant men for 3-6 months and see what happens. I give them 24 hours, and they would be sneaking back to their nice houses with protection. In fact, they would probably pay for body doubles, ok, who would do that job? Or perhaps we could get KierCo to share the same all-inclusive hotels as the illegals? Let's be honest that's exactly what politicians are doing to the public and have been for many years, is that ok? No, but should they not be leading by example? The village of Wethersfield in Essex knows only too well about the impact. They have groups of young men walking across private land defecating in public areas, fields and lanes, they have no regard for the villagers or their way of life. Many of the locals feel threatened, no surprise. But what will the Police do – probably nothing.

Stopping Illegal and Managing Legal immigration

Despite politicians spouting off about how difficult it is to stop immigration, it's a relatively simple thing to do, rather than dreaming up elaborate schemes. We have had Rishi with his £80m Marcon deal in 2022 followed by the Rhwanda deal, which did appear to have a positive impact on numbers for a very short time. We have had 'smash the smugglers' from Keir and more recently a £500 million 'stop the boats' in France and a few tweaks to the pathetic immigration law/policy which will fall on deaf ears to the smugglers. We have even had the justice secretary say illegals breaking the Law will be deported, wow! they are here illegally so they should all be deported. So, let's look at a few simple solutions:

- Stop the freebies – their perks; the private health care; nice meals and hotel rooms; free phones etc. all the benefits. I do not know of any other European country that provides such benefits. There are thousands of illegals all over Europe who sleep in parks and try to work and find food during the day. The city of Milan in Italy is the most striking example I have seen. There is no free stuff. The locals and authorities do not look favourably on them, and they are well contained by the threat of the authorities.

- Change the law so the illegal entrants cannot use silly excuses to stay and demand benefits – that's not tweaking the law; it's interpreting/ignoring elements of the European Human Rights Act and International Law. Create a new emergency law that puts the UK first, built on zero tolerance to Illegals. As part of the new law, significantly tighten the criteria for issuing visas and citizenship to the UK.

- No benefits (income support, housing, healthcare, pension) legal immigrants until you have worked and paid NI/Tax for a minimum of 5-7 Years. Introduce a cooling off and assessment period of 10-12 years, which must be passed; if not, they get sent home. Also, the assessment should be carried out on an individual basis, so they wouldn't just be able to bring their family over with them and get benefits on arrival. Now if you wanted to make a difficult decision Mr or Mrs Politician, then here is your chance. Say there are elements of these laws that the UK refuses to accept and implement a zero-tolerance approach, now that's a difficult decision.

- A treatment plan for the individuals already here is, close the hotels, set up 6-10 holding centres, controlled by the military with support from a retrained/repurposed immigration team. We have expertise in creating temporary sites for thousands of people. A three-year return plan should be put in place. Illegals should be put to work while waiting to be returned (a form of National Service). There are plenty of jobs, repairing potholes, litter picking, cleaning road signs. Those who refuse to work should be prioritised to go home first. The appeal process should be stopped immediately and people on it returned to their country of origin without question. If these countries refuse then stop issuing visas, as Robert Jenrick suggested.

- We pay our taxes/bills to live, by working. So why should illegals be exempt? At present, it seems like favouritism for illegals over the working class of the UK. The core principle to adopt is whilst you're being processed to return home, pay your way and be put to work.

- The Boats- Step 1, distribute/handout leaflets in the camps in France and across Europe, and bombard social media telling the illegals of the new rules and that the boats will have their engines disabled and they will be towed back to whence they came from.

- Step 2, Have a joint French and British military force along the coastline, putting roadblocks/check points in place on all entry points to the beaches. This would be supported by drone fly zones to spot the incoming smugglers so they can be intercepted. Drones do fly at night you know.

- Tough action, a no-nonsense approach to immigration is needed. We have zero control of legal and illegal immigration. That is a fact. We could certainly learn a lot from countries who seek to protect their people from the negative economic impact and terrorist threat that immigration clearly brings. The lack of taking tough and decisive action is not uncommon in the UK with the political parties we have had over the years- weak and spineless.

Taking a zero-tolerance approach would benefit the UK so much, no housing crisis; reduced NHS waiting lists; reduced crime; citizens feeling safer; reduced burden on our infrastructure; better public services etc, and with an estimated £75-£100bn a year saving maybe a tax cut. Yes, a government that actually wants to improve something for its citizens and give back is so badly needed – now there's a thought. We must appreciate that stopping immigration will not solve all the issues the UK has, but it would be a bloody good start.

Snowballing Monster

When talking of immigration there tends to be a focus on one or two areas, the ever-increasing numbers due to the daily taxi service from France to the UK or the French police turning a blind eye etc. Seeing the big picture is difficult so the media and government use certain data points. However, there needs to be more focus on the monster the politicians have created. It's like a horror film, an alien comes to earth and starts to eat people and natural resources as it consumes it grows ever larger and unstoppable. In the movie we have patriotic heroes who then kill off the alien after a major battle. I love Marvel MCU! Meanwhile, back on earth to the UK in 2025, the political elite have created something very similar. Rather than deal with immigration head on, they have allowed the creation of a circular industry (monster) that constantly feeds itself with more immigrants and it becomes increasingly larger, consuming pretty much everything in its wake. I have highlighted the extensive list of resources to support it previously and it is incredulous and pathetic that politicians have allowed it to grow and grow. To stop the snowballing monster, isn't the answer obvious?

Legals Vs Aliens

Many of my friends are working legal immigrants; Polish; South African; Latvian; Thai; Malaysian; Burmese; Indian, and they are also growing angrier, not so much against the individuals, more the stupidity and incompetence of the UK government doing nothing and accepting it as the norm. All of them have followed the lengthy, very costly process to obtain their right to live and work as a UK Citizen. These friends are the right type of immigrants paying taxes and contributing like any other worker in the UK. Interestingly they do not see the rejection and animosity towards the illegals as racist (sorry lefties), quite the opposite. Their view is that it's common sense to reject the illegals. They are asking, "Why would you let these people just walk into your country and get everything for free while your own people struggle and suffer?" An example my Polish friend used was, "If you paid money to have a private party with food and drink and ten young men turned up who you didn't know, walked in and started eating and drinking your food, molesting the women and children in front of you, is that ok? No, it's not, and it's simply not racist to kick them out and have the police prosecute them - what is wrong with your government and the authorities in the UK?" Most of them are surprised that there isn't more protest from the UK citizens and are struggling to understand why this country does not stick up for itself. Politicians really should take heed of this view, because unless the situation changes soon all of them will take their cash and go home and we will lose more skilled workers who contribute positively to the UK. My friends came to the UK to prosper and be a part of what Great Britian used to be. Now they feel that they are being taken advantage of. The exodus will happen in the next 2-3 years, I see many UK citizens doing the same.

The Law is An Ass, and it Continues To Be – Beware

No Law No Order

Law and order agencies are supposed to be a core pillar of our country, we should trust them and if we feel we are not safe we should be able to go to them as a safe haven to seek help and support from bad people. We have all seen and heard the shocking headlines about crime, over the last few decades crime has soared upward year on year. Are we in the UK the Wild West or a third world country where real criminals just do what they want and take what they want with little or no consequence? Sometimes it's hard to tell. Look at the total mess in any major city across the UK, especially London. There doesn't seem to be a day that goes by without some horrific incident, crime after crime, drugs everywhere, stabbing after stabbing. Crime is rife. The evidence of criminals blatantly flouting the law is reported daily and nothing changes. The murders of Lee Rigby, Olivia Pratt-Korbel and Khayri Mclean; the latter murdered in broad daylight as he walked home. These are just a few shocking examples. Crimes involving people (neighbours, family, friends, regular citizens) are heavily impacted. Many do not feel safe on the streets or if they tell the police, nothing seems to happen. Crime on the street involving regular folk is where the biggest increase has occurred, clearly demonstrating to me a left wing and woke attitude of the authorities towards the people who want to commit a crime. Worst of all, the victim is so rarely compensated with a fitting verdict and sentence from the broken, corrupt legal system. The justice system is in trouble and in need of a complete review/overhaul of the court process. That's not just convicting people of wrongdoing but also correcting errors of justice in a much more efficient/effective way. The CPS plays a big role in the justice system and the people in charge need to be accountable for their blunders. According to Dominic Casciani of the BBC in Feb 2023 there were 61,737 serious crime cases outstanding. That simply tells me that the people running have no clue how to manage a backlog. More importantly, why is there a backlog in the first place?

I was always under the impression that in the UK you were innocent until proven guilty, however, justice in the UK favours the large corporates, government bodies and financial institutions with their army of lawyers, people of power on their boards. Yes, money and who you know, talks in the legal system. Taking on a big business or the government in any shape or form is practically an impossibility. They have big pockets lined with money to hire top lawyers- King's Counsels on speed dial, should there be a problem from a member of the public.

Everyone is entitled to a fair trial, but people in general need help navigating their way around an antiquated and extremely complicated set of laws, processes, procedures and system, which has been deliberately put in place over the centuries to keep the uneducated and poorer public in their place, or of course jail.

Have you ever wondered why the legal firms earn such good money? I have met many lawyers and none of them struggle to pay their bills Meanwhile the average citizen who falls between wealth and criminality is constantly overlooked and churned through the system and spat out, if they are unfortunate enough to get caught up in it. The Crown Prosecution Service (CPS) acts more like a gangster organisation playing a conviction numbers game rather than using a moral compass and common sense or acting in the interests of the country/community.

CPS - Guilty until Proven Innocent

The Crown Prosecution Service, according to their website, gives a clear indication of what their role is in society and the benefits us as citizens should expect for the price tag of £500-£600 million a year:

The CPS prosecutes independently, fairly and works to deliver justice in every case and act in the interest of the pubic.

However, the government CPS.gov.uk website appears to have many contradictions. It works closely and advises the police, it also states that it helps victims and witnesses implying it has already made up its mind at the outset. Quite a contradiction.

After speaking to several lawyers, barristers and spending time observing cases put before the Magistrates and Crown Court, justice in many cases is a fudge, because the law is so complicated/old and in many cases retrofitted to the current day. If you are unfortunate to be on the receiving end of a prosecution from the CPS you will realise that you are considered guilty before entering the court room, you will have to prove your innocence. The CPS and the police seem to be joined at the hip and collaborate to get results. The former also bows to the current political tune driven by woke and EDI agendas. We must have more rape conviction, well what if there are no rape cases to answer, but let's try hard to find some. That's not acting independently in my book that's divisive, sinister and totally wrong. Tactics for hitting numbers, coupled with year-on-year backlogs, I must ask the question, "Is everyone getting a fair trial?", the level of overturned convictions in recent years strongly supports that argument.

Tip of the Iceberg

The CPS will pick up cases even if the complainant (so called victim) does not want to press charges, because they were either acting illegally themselves and are solely or partially the reason the incident happened in the first instance. Also, the CPS and police when it suits them ignore the person that broke the law in the first instance, this happens in many cases of self-defence, someone breaks into your house, you defend yourself. A kind of embarrassment if you like - causing a fight is a culpable act but then blaming the person who defends themselves and gets a jail sentence- how is that fair? Yes, you did just read that last two sentences. The CPS take it upon themselves to be the unwanted Lone Ranger upholding the law for the so called good of the public, but is it? I observed a case in the Crown Court. In summary a young man with a baby and his pregnant wife were on their way home one evening in the car. There was a van blocking the single lane road illegally. The van man was offloading furniture into his home, he deliberately ignored the young man and made him wait for some time, when he did move the van man gave the finger to the young man. The young man tooted the van man. The van man got out of the van, ran down the road and hit the young man's car, punched the window all the time shouting obscenity to the young man and his family in the car. The young man got out of the car believing he and his family were clearly under threat and in immediate danger. He did not want to drive away in fear he may run van man over or pull out into a main road and crash the car with his family in. Van man then attacked the young man; the young man did what most people would do in that situation, defended himself. Both were injured, van man more than the young man. A tragic set of circumstances that ended in the crown court. However, the young man, put in a dangerous and unnecessary situation with his family, was charged and faces a hefty jail sentence because it's apparently in the public's interest to prosecute him-say the CPS. Yet van man instigated and provoked the situation in the first place and admitted the injuries he received were his fault, and apparently, initially did not want to prosecute the young man. Subsequently, van man was not charged even though he broke the law three times before the fisty cuffs started. Make your own mind up. The most disgraceful part which shows how much contempt the CPS has for real justice, is that they made no attempt to reference the vulnerable baby or the pregnant woman who were traumatised by the so-called victim. In fact, they claimed the young man was on his own and was a mute - nor did they make their evidence available until the very last minute (conveniently losing some of it) to help the defence have a fair trial. What I witnessed was a total travesty, a game, theatre, not a fair trial. I was shocked, it is no surprise people have lost trust.

On a much bigger scale than the young man above, to prove the question of incompetence across the legal system, let's look at two recent cases. Before I launch into it, I want to remind readers that whatever I write next can be argued in some way or another as incorrect by the Police or CPS as they are in charge?! In the same way politicians are never wrong and never really lie or over promise. So:

The Lucy Letby trial was a complete whitewash; she is guilty because killing babies in anyone's book is beyond terrible and because it was deemed so by the CPS and the legal system long before the trial. It was never going to be easy when the media coverage started with her arrest for the whole country to see. I may have mis-read Lucy's look, but she looked in shock. It's a horrific crime and Lucy deserves her 15 life sentences, if she truly did it. Since the conviction, increasingly more mistakes from the holier than thou CPS and Police have come to light. Basic evidence that was apparently not dealt with appropriately, and specialists predicting outcomes that may or may not be relevant at all. Nor, it would appear, have the context/circumstances of working on a neonatal ward been correctly or adequately portrayed, which basically means it was not considered by the jury – fair trial? Average death rates, comparisons with other similar neonatal wards, there is plenty of relevant research out there. A well measured article by Nadine Dorries in the Mail (4/2/25), highlights many of these anomalies and discrepancies. Just from a common-sense perspective it raises suspicion in how the CPS managed the trial, particularly the use of the so-called expert. In fact, the CPS choice of expert was not so in neonatal medicine and the evidence Dr Evans used to address the jury was someone else's, who was the expert? So, Dr Evans might have well been a GP reading out and interpreting someone else's work - wow. It's also clear that Lucy was not left alone on every occasion, perhaps there are many of her colleagues who do not believe she is guilty, that was 2024. Now it's 2025, February in fact and a panel of neonatal experts have done what the CPS should have done initially, which is look for the TRUTH, not just try and fix the outcome to get their numbers up. The panel of experts have confirmed that Lucy is not guilty of the crimes she has been convicted for, but the victim of multiple failings by the prosecution.

In contrast to the above, when the CPS and Police have a known (beyond doubt) killer with a potted track record as long as your arm, they go all soft. The Nottingham Attacks and the events leading up to the murder of 3 innocent victims beg belief. There was blatant failing of the government owned authorities to do their job. The murders could clearly have been prevented. Consequently, after the trial, the families received more bad news when a seemingly light touch sentence was given to murderer Valdo Calocane. On Sky (2025) one of the mothers, Emma Webber gave her side of the story, sighting specific failings from the Nottingham, Leicestershire Police, Nottingham mental health trust and the CPS. Emma is a strong woman; however, her frustration is totally and utterly understandable. I commend her and the other victims' families for standing up and shouting out loud for what is right and just. The failing of the authorities prior to the attacks was almost accepted as the norm, the verdict and punishment seem totally disproportionate, and a number of folks on the government payroll should be sacked and held to account publicly. There will be an inquiry, but so what, we will waste a lot of taxpayers' money to ascertain what we already know and with other inquiries we will confirm, it could have been prevented, a few changes will be made, tick the box. What is really needed, as a minimum, is for the people responsible to lose their job and/or face prosecution themselves. That would start to focus the minds of the establishment on being responsible and accountable, rather than just taking from the public coffers and doing half a job.

In addition to this, we have the following shocking and unthinkable U-turn, a total miscarriage of justice. The Peter Sullivan case. Unfortunately, this is only a tip of the iceberg. His appeal took far too long and that's disgraceful-I bet no one gets the sack. It should come as no surprise that there is no respect for the legal circus in the UK.

The underlying problem with the CPS, Police and legal system is, it is not fair, transparent or honest. Their job, so it would seem, is to tell the tale that they want to tell you (the jury), and anything that does not support the conviction, they don't like to share. It's like a parent paraphrasing a child's bed time story because they want their child to sleep, tell them the good bits and ignore the detail of why- Snow White was rescued by the prince and lived happy ever after... .The Police are supposed to have a legal obligation to look at all the evidence, even if it leads them away from their chosen line of inquiry, but they often tailor the evidence to suit their argument, because they work with the CPS, some say joined at the hip, on a game of odds. Irrespective of all the legal BS and justification the CPS give, for me there are more holes in Lucy's trial then in your average kitchen sieve. As with the Nottingham stabbings, there was not enough focus on the accused's real state of mind, which lead to the light touch sentence in hospital. However, the chance of a fair trial, or all the truth being fully declared, especially when it's the establishment, is few and far between. That's supposedly the legal system looking after the public's interest?

These cases and circumstances I have outlined are a tip of the Iceberg. The LawGazette.co.uk (June 2013) points out that two Crown Court Judges had criticised the CPS for their incompetence supporting a murder trial, the other a rape case and making simple mistakes cataloguing who came and went on the nursing ward in the Lucy Letby case. They are now refusing to provide detailed information regarding their prosecution, that will probably just get lost in the post. The CPS seem to have contempt for the people they are supposed to represent, i.e. the victims and the accused, in order to conduct a fair trial. It would appear that they don't like complaints either as they have a big problem dealing with them according to The Standard (23/8/23). Its own watchdog has basically told it to get a grip. Theguardian.com highlighted the CPS' difficulty in disclosing documents to defendants and the presentation of the true facts. This is a growing trend with many examples. This unprofessional behaviour, however, brings me back in some way to the young man's case I observed above, disclosure and presenting all the evidence in a timely manner or saying they had lost evidence was not on the CPS task list pre-trial. No, the young man's barrister was told the day the trial started.

The CPS' response to these claims will not surprise you, like all badly run government departments, it cites a lack of funding. Is a lack of funding an excuse for wrongly convicting someone or letting a real criminal go free? This is total incompetence; poor excuses and bad management are standard fair with criticising a government funded authority. The comment from Max Hill QC, Director of Public Prosecutions, frames the CPS' lack of experience and competence, by saying that the extra £85m funding they received would help them recruit more prosecutors to solve the disclosure issues. I think that's the last thing they should spend the money on; getting organised, better governance; creating a more honest, fair and transparent culture and process; and attention to detail would be far better choices. Thats what the CPS is supposed to stand for – impartiality/neutrality ensuring everyone gets a fair trial. These are clearly not what prosecutors and judges are good at, nor should they be. Their job is to administer and follow the law and code by which they apparently operate, but that is not sufficient, other skills need to be blended into the process with good leadership. And no, that does not mean hanging out at the Christmas party, shmoozing with politicians or the Police. This maverick organisation needs changing fast, it has the stench of bias towards its core values and all that it purports to be.

Casino Court Room

In the Crown Court, one of the most concerning and totally contradictive things about the Law is majority voting. The law was established on the use of a jury of 12 good women and men being beyond reasonable doubt that a crime had been committed, if all agree then the verdict is guilty, if they cannot agree, they are free to leave, agreement being 100% sure. Then the meddling politicians in 1967 decided that given the population of the time and probably empty prisons, not enough people were being prosecuted, so they introduced Majority Voting. Majority Voting is an 80% 'are you sure?' vote, basically the judge will accept 10 to 2 as guilty after a period. My observation is that it helps the CPS numbers game; it means judges can wrap cases up more quickly and gives the jury an early finish on a Friday afternoon, if they have been in court since Monday. This is all in the name of fair justice.

I always thought that finding out and telling the Truth was the foundation of Law and society in general, having a fair trial is essential to our democracy and separates us from third world dictatorship and communist countries. However, my experience tells me the legal system and many of the people who operate it simply don't care, or at least their words don't match their actions. Victims are distraught; people have their lives ruined when wrongly convicted and the compensation scheme is woeful. The system needs a massive overhaul. For them it's a numbers game, appeasing the political tune of the day. What about Justice for the people – it's like betting your life on Red or Black?

Lack of respect for the police

It is fair to say that some police forces and the individuals who work for the police haven't done themselves any favours in recent times. We know it's a tough job, we all get that, but there have been contradictions and many blunders not only on a national level but on our streets too- basic keystone cop stuff. South Yorkshire Police and the Hillsborough cover up is one example, or the disaster dealing with the hundreds of victims in Rotherham who were continually abused by Asian gangs, and many others. They have not only come under scrutiny from their own governing body, but much of the public simply doesn't trust them.

Police forces are there to enforce the law, fairly and free from political bias. They used to be a trusted pillar of society upholding what was right. If you had an issue, you would go to the police as a safe organisation that would assist you and ensure your safety. However, more recently they are seen as a face of the interfering government, and a lot of anger, resistance and confrontation is expressed towards them from the public at large. For example, the MPS or Met have chosen two tier policing driven by the political agenda of Cresa Dick and now, Sir Mark Rowley. Mark clearly seems to have political bias towards the left and minority groups rather than anything British. This was clearly demonstrated when poppy fund-raising volunteers were told by Met officers not to promote Armistice Day. Apparently, it would upset and offend the pro-Palestine protesting thugs or call the thousands of people who turned up to see Tommy Robinson's speech in Parliament square, far right extremists, funny there was no real trouble at that event. Mark, be a policeman and do your job, park the left-wing agenda/liberal compass or is it your boss Mr Khan and his boss Mr Starmer heavily influencing your judgement? We do have to remember that the government pays the wages and the big benefits package the police receive. However, what is the benefit of this interference? If there are more complaints, people feel unsafe and harbour a lack of trust in the police. Has left wing interference benefited UK citizens?

The most recent example of two-tier policing is the comparison between the treatment of the rioting crowd (2024) and so-called thuggery in Southport and organised crime at the Notting Hill Carnival in 2024. Very similar claims of criminal damage, disorder and attacks on the police were reported, but I did not see Kier march the Notting Hill offenders off to special evening courts with maximum sentences dished out. The reality is that the politicians will put a different spin on it to suit their tune. The rioting thugs made the Labour look stupid (that's not difficult), so they got the full brunt of the law under instruction of the ex-CPS man Starmer. Yet the organised (probably many known to the police) criminals and thugs (attempted rape and murder on the list) got the lighter end of the law for some strange reason. Most people can't reason this contradictory nonsense, the same laws should apply to all, but perhaps not in the UK, with its biased political agendas?

Being a police officer has never been easy. Not only because of social media and the challenges that it brings in terms of constant scrutiny, political interference which brings more red tape, ticking boxes and form filling, no it's the law and the system that is putting the pressure on the police and criminals know exactly how to use it against them. Their job must get tougher every day given the cultural Armageddon and political left-wing slant we are all witnessing - two tier policing needs to stop.

They fail to attend burglaries, probably too busy watching screens and tweets, camera watching for that very dangerous criminal, the speeding motorist-really! Doing paperwork, ticking boxes and being TV celebrities on channel 5, while children are stabbed to death, "Trust us." they say. Why would we?

In the courts

Plea bargaining starts at the outset (this is apparently illegal in the UK). If you plead guilty in the first instance there is a 30% reduction in your sentence, you then return to court and have another chance to plead guilty, but as you didn't the first time, it's reduced to 20%, depending on what you are in court for- what nonsense. It should make no difference, the same sentence for a crime should apply. The plea-bargaining tool (my interpretation) is used to reduce sentences because there is not enough space in the prisons. So, whilst you might be guilty, by admitting it early you're doing us a favour. I struggle with the fairness and incentive if a person truly believes they are innocent. Criminal cases, irrespective of the plea still go-ahead, what is the point of admitting that you're guilty, when we still waste taxpayer's money doing the trial. Again depending on what the crime is.

There is so much bureaucracy and time wasting in courts, the level of support that a judge needs is amazing. There were between 6-8 people supporting a judge and the court, not many of them doing much to be honest. Then you have the prosecutor and defendant lawyer/barrister- if the accused is lucky to have one- and the individual on trial. That seems excessive to me. There is so much scope for streamlining the justice system. If people plead guilty why put them on trial, there could easily be a set of standard measures applied to certain type of cases. Or why do you have to go to a magistrate's court to enter a plea, when the magistrate's court is too junior to handle certain criminal cases? They simply flick it to the Crown Court, why bother with the magistrates? Go straight to the Crown Court. Removing the time wasting and inefficiencies would one get rid of the year-on-year backlogs, save millions, but more importantly prevent the emotional stress for the victim and defendant who have their lives torn apart waiting for a trial. Furthermore, the conduct of some judges and magistrates when speaking to defendants is questionable- disrespectful, dismissive, outright rude. Every human being should be treated equally, after all it's their life and in many cases their families who bear the brunt of a conviction. Have a little respect judge. One day we are all judged. How would you like to be treated? The more damaging aspect of this behaviour in front of a jury is that it supports the prosecution's case and it could and probably does wrongly influence the jury to a guilty verdict. The jury in some cases will take direction from the judge, especially in a complex or sensitive circumstance where there is no clear way to arrive at a verdict. If that's the case, it should be thrown out and not pursued.

Almost all courts are in the public domain. You would not think this when you enter the court building. There is more security per person than at your average airport, although in courts my experience is that the security team are much more polite, but entering as a member of the public can be daunting. Apparently, the reason for the security is to protect the court staff, solicitors, barristers and witnesses. So, if the justice system is fair and transparent why are so many people playing up and putting people's security at risk? The obvious answer would be, because it's the accused or their associates that kick off when they are convicted. There is always an element of that for sure and there will always be people that react inappropriately and are not happy. However, I have a different answer. I have talked about the CPS, the state of the justice system, lack of transparency and fairness overall and the attitude and absence of quality policing in our neighbourhoods. Whether you are a victim or the accused, being exposed to these behaviours will only frustrate you and make you angry; in addition, you must wait a long time to say your piece. In my opinion, the uprising and lack of trust is because of what the police, CPS and legal system have created. Another group of government organisations that squanders taxpayers' cash, with a clear inability to focus on the right things that matter to the public and society at large. Adding to that, the lack of accountability we consistently see more of, yet no one gets fired, and consequently nothing changes.

Turning the law on its head

Clearly the Law and the system that supports it need to change fast, and I mean fast, to give people back the confidence and trust it should have. What's needed is a downgrading of laws that are disproportionate in favour of power, money, corporate business and government. An introduction of laws with much stricter consequences to protect and are in favour of innocent public. This is where the majority of crime has increased. The hardships the public face are drug, knife, domestic, burglary, and gang related, as well as other forms of violent crime. 'Protect the people, not the establishment', needs to the way forward to bring society back in line. The whole process needs to be made efficient, it's out-dated.

Some suggested law changes:

- Introduce a minimum 20-year sentence for carrying or using a knife for crime. If a knife is wielded in public and the police attend, then officers should be allowed to shoot and kill the perpetrator.
- A very strong message needs to be sent to the youth too. Stop protecting criminals who are underage from being named. If they are old enough to commit a crime, then they are old enough to face the consequences and be named, as a minimum. Now 16-year-olds can vote, surely, they can be named.
- More law to reflect society to-day.
- If prisoners are not prepared to rehabilitate inside prison, then they should be put to work alongside the lazy illegals who are crossing the channel.
- Stop treating people with mental health issues any different from other criminals. If you commit a crime, it's still a crime and the punishment should be the same.

Crime has escalated out of control in the last 20 years, because there is no control or real consequences for real criminals. With ever more people walking into the UK minus any form of identification or background check, it will simply add to the problem.

Julie Rothchild

Just Throwing Random Ingredients Together Can Leave a Bad Taste in Your Mouth, or a Violent Reaction

Cleansing of the UK Culture

Culture can be defined as ' people's learned beliefs, values and behaviours. In the UK this is founded upon Christian values that came massively into play after World War I and II. Society being polite – well-mannered and friendly, respecting yourself and being respectful to your neighbours, helping others, live and let live. This was in turn reciprocated by those whom you encountered across the UK, residents and other people who supported the UK during the challenge of war time. Everyone in turn prospered from the experience, acceptance and community wealth creation. This coupled with the slight right political slant of the late 60s- early 90s gave us structure, purpose and clear direction as a nation. The UK was respected by the rest of the World, a leader on the international stage. The UK was a leading example of a strong culture, with decent people and was considered a safe place to live. We led from the front and were proud and patriotic.

The first 35 years of my life, I have to say that's what I experienced; this great culture, visiting friends, family and holidaying across the UK, meeting new people who shared and reciprocated like for like, everyone seemed to benefit from our culture. Travelling abroad was also amazing; everyone was keen to associate and talk to me because I was from the UK. Yes, the UK citizens worked hard, people respected themselves and others, crime rates were low, it was a more satisfying existence. So, what went wrong? Well, then Blair's term started in government and the journey to decay accelerated. The last 30 years or so have been very different, the core values and pleasant culture we once had, have been eroded year on year. The minority appear to have a bigger voice than the majority now. Things have deteriorated more quickly than I could ever have imagined. Yes, I am sure that there are a few small but isolated bolt holes or bubbles left in the UK, but it's an ever-decreasing number as our county has become a saturated and overpopulated mish- mash, where our own (UK) citizens are constantly overlooked. The elite of our country, not surprisingly have been totally and utterly complacent, pushing onto us poorly thought through local and national policies and laws, not to maintain or uphold the UK culture, but to destroy it and replace it with something very liberal and dangerous. I would encourage people to visit some of Britain's inner cities, parts of Birmingham; Leicester: Nottingham, and London, where some communities and streets bear no physical resemblance to the UK or its culture and the first language is definitely not English.

The cultural impact on normal people's life is significant. Illegal immigrants are pushed into communities with little thought to the cultural difference there in and left to manage with virtually no support. If the authorities have done such an exemplary job, why are there more than 1 million people in the UK speaking little or no English according to the 2021 census reported in the Mail (Daily Mail 6/3/25)? That figure will have ballooned by now as overall rates have increased since 2021. Just to be clear, English is still the national language of the UK - for now.

Good and bad culture is normally learned at a subliminal level by example in society to follow. Good role models and strong leaders are an extremely important and needed in the UK today, more so for young men who need a sense of belonging and who need to know the boundaries. It's not a surprise that more young men and now women are joining gangs and committing crime as part of their everyday life. In gangs the rules are simple and straightforward, and they make sense because it's a level playing field, break the rules and you face punishment, play the game and you are rewarded. Some will say that's how it is in normal life, but is it? Not for many youngsters. Punishment and reward in the normal world depend upon who you are and who you know, it is not fair nor straightforward it's just blurred with no clarity, and the elite decide. The I newspaper (I 2/1/23) ran an article on teachers being concerned about 'alpha male' influences on boys. They cite Andrew Tate as an example, saying that boys are becoming 'more disrespectful and defiant toward them'. Well again it's very easy to blame someone else isn't it and deflect away from the real problem? I have listened to school workers who have been attacked by pupils who wreck classrooms, they are as young as 5 and 6; teachers can't do anything to stop them. These kids have never heard of Andrew Tate. The issue with these young children is the lack of firm, fair discipline; where are the male role models one asks? What about giving the parent more responsibility for their children, rather than giving the child the power in the family? Why are teachers potty training children and being the only line of accountability for them? Society has become so weak; are parents still parents? Also, the white male is constantly being undermined and persecuted by the woke community. So, what do you expect? It's not Andrew Tate's fault, is it? Has anyone actually charged him for anything, proved anything or prosecuted him yet? No, I thought not. The authorities just don't like his narrative, and he calls them out as dumb, stupid and he is right, that's why they keep making stuff up to arrest him. How about asking the education secretary Bridget Phillipson? That's if you can get hold of her on her four-day week working from home! Youngsters will look towards characters like Andrew Tate, Jeremy Clarkson and Nigel Farage because they lead, tell it how it is and take a pop at what is wrong with the establishment's liberal attitude. They don't dress everything up as perfect with rose-tinted glasses. The truth can be an ugly place, so calling it out and making it better is what counts for many youngsters. The problem is the politicians don't like the truth.

Out of sight out of mind

The cultural impact for all people's life is significant because of immigration and the general decline of values across the UK. The basic plan has been to scatter illegals who have been granted asylum and some who haven't, into our communities, cities and towns with little thought or strategy. It seems the core principle of cultural integration is 'Be like me and be better' What this means is that immigrants get put into a place with normal UK citizens, they then will befriend a hardworking, taxing paying, law abiding neighbour, learn from them and reflect the core values of our culture similar to a UK person. Yep, they become a great British citizen, and Great Britain continues to flourish. Stop there, spoiler alert. It's been proven many times that when you mix different people together with little thought or consideration for their culture, the outcome is never a good one and it becomes a downward spiral and crime increases. I remember my own experience when I lived on a new council estate in London, you had to be a good rent payer to the Greater London Council (GLC) for at least two years to qualify for accommodation on this new estate. After a few years past the GLC under Red Labour, Ken Livingstone had housing issues to manage, some prompted by a surge in immigration. Ken and the central government, with little thought, crushed different people and cultures together. As a resident it became a race to the bottom and the deterioration was rapid. Within approximately 12 months, everyone we knew had left the estate and I was not far behind. Vandalism and crime were rife. Women and children were scared to go out, the council even blocked two walkways that connected the flats, to help improve safety. Just before I left, the drug dealers and users moved in, and the estate was condemned, to be torn down some years later. Being part of that immigration experiment was very uncomfortable and unnecessary. However, I did feel for some of the elderly and young families who had to endure it for many years. When will the government and councils learn that mixing people with completely different views/culture is not beneficial and it creates animosity?

It would seem that these days the nation and its culture are more like dog eat dog; survival of the fittest; less regard for people in general; respect has gone out of the window; fewer people care. All the factors outlined in this book contribute to third world attitudes- individual values and behaviours have all declined. Yes, there are still well mannered and polite people. Families who are doing their best to bring up their children to be rounded, grounded and good citizens, but the situation is not joyful, it's more like an outright battle with woke nonsense, authorities and public services failing you. For many parents it's becoming increasingly difficult the absolute moral fabric is being stretched thinner by the day, under normal conditions; the pain of travelling anywhere by car or train, flooding in the winter, drought in the summer; increasingly more money picked out of your pocket by the tax man, corporate UK overcharging us for everything and the government doing nothing. The media are relentless in reporting this. After a while people become numb and attempt to switch off to the noise. They are fed up and angry. That anger is kept inside because freedom of expression and speech is slowly being removed unless you are one of the privileged woke crowd who seems to be permitted to say whatever they want. So, it appears that we are turning on each other rather than focusing on who is to blame, the folk in number 10.

The immigration service has failed to integrate so called refugees/illegals into our society. The UK culture is fast disappearing because we have allowed them to establish the same environment from whence, they came, and it is simply replicated here in the UK. The outcome from this crashing of cultures in this way is regressive on every level as these people do not contribute in the same way UK citizens do. The outcome should be progressive, work hard, reduce crime, pay your way, be respectful. Sadly, that's not what I see.

Eco Numpties – Stop What

Another extreme reflection on the culture in the UK is 'just stop oil' (JSO). It really doesn't matter how you categorise this crowd, whether you call them Eco Zealots, Eco Numpties or outright disgraceful. They are either privileged and/or thick with, poorly thought through ideals and very selfish; that's why this toxic combination of attributes makes this bunch so messed up and unaccountable for their actions. There are a lot of them and like a secret organisation they appear to have a wide range of members and sympathisers in very high places. Destroy, disrupt and create havoc wherever we go is their mantra, this is backward thinking. Their random tactics have not been seen since the 16th-17th century where mobs rule on the streets in the main cities. When the first attacks started, we were all surprised and angered. However, the first few roadblocks and paint spraying incidents saw the authorities, police and the courts respond slowly to this threat, almost sympathising with their cause. If you went around vandalising Harrods, the Bank of England, New Scotland Yard office, MI5 building or damaging a Van Gogh painting worth £76m, you would be fined and locked up for a long time. No, no, the elite and privileged in society continue to take time to act, as if to deliberately allow them space and more time to create havoc, to annoy and disrupt the public further. It's only when the public reached breaking point and started to act, grapple and fight back, (do the police's job), that the authorities and courts started to take it seriously. Again, another example of the state showing contempt for the public and their everyday lives. Yes, some of the Eco Mob have been convicted and a few minor sentences dished out based upon out-of-dated laws that don't fit the crime. To top that, more of the wealthy, privileged acting community came out in sympathy and objected to the length of the sentence. If you were to ask the people who have been considerably inconvenienced and lost income, they would have a very different view. Clearly the acting community were not impacted by any of the disruption they created whilst on their private jets.

JSO actions are plain and simple - social and domestic terrorism and should be treated as such. The mob have started to change tactics becoming more brazen as the consequence for action certainly does not deter them. Similar to drug addicts going from Marijuana to Cocaine to Heroin to total criminal junky, they just can't stop or won't stop. The habit has taken over. They have started to target politician's houses. I suspect personal attacks on certain public figures will follow, like throwing orange milk shake or egg at them, but ultimately physical harm will ensue. New measures and laws are needed to tackle this new form of terrorism against UK citizens and the country. It needs to happen quickly before it escalates and ends in tragedy. I do condone people taking action and doing what they think is right and objecting peacefully. JSO crowd are simply posh left-wing mobsters and vandals and should be dealt with in the same way as the rioters or people using violence.

The JSO action has now stalled (not before time) and we have the Palestine Action group. This group clearly didn't like the London Pride Parade hurling paint amongst other things and blocking roads, I wonder why they are at odds with Pride? I suspect half the people protesting for this group glued themselves to the motorway trunk roads over the last couple of years. Maybe rent a mob, some of them look like the same people though! The cultural impact is less about what these people stand for, because we have been here before, (I support people expressing their views peacefully and in turn accepting other's views – free speech) the damage to our culture is that the authorities continue to allow it to happen on our streets and it never tends to end up peacefully. The type of protesters we have seen of late, mirror images of the third world rebellion we have witnessed across Africa and Asia.

There was a chap called Guy Fawkes, who had a mob of people trying to impart their strong religious views on Protestant folk. It was unwelcome at the time and didn't get very far with the normal forms of protest. In an act of desperation in 1605 he decided to try and blow up the houses of parliament. History often repeats itself; it won't be long, I suspect.

The Four Horsemen plus Z and Z+

So, the Four Horsemen of the Apocalypse is a Biblical tale and represents the four characteristics that lead to the end of mankind, in the form of Conquest; War; Famine and Death. On a global scale we can see this playing out again. Putin's war in the Ukraine, Gazza, famine in India and Africa et al. With all these things and a splash of Covid, death is the next step. We have seen a lot of it. Wow! Look how far we have come as a civilisation, technology and science, did a man actually land on the moon in 1966? However, there are still many woes around the world, and they do not seem to be improving. How long has there been famine in certain African states. The war in Gazza seems to have gone on my entire life. At the heart of all these woes and issues sits politics in the broadest sense. But it's also taking shape on a micro level in the UK. Toss in the behaviours of generation Z, a dose of far-left liberalism to numb the brains of the many, and the future looks pretty bleak.

Generation Z are people born between 1987 and 2012. Rather than age, their behaviours are the clearest indication of a Z status (Zda's). Classic behaviours from my perspective, for much of this generation is; full of entitlement; they struggle to converse with other generations; have their head buried in a phone or games consols most of the time; struggle with reality; not responsible or accountable for their actions and shocking at time keeping, the list goes on. However, there are the copycat Zda's who do not fit the age bracket but do mirror the behaviours. These are the Z+ generation who are even easier to spot. 'the older generation aged 40-60 who are dumb and incapable of putting down their phones.' You have seen them out at dinner in a restaurant, unable to hold a conversation with their partner, or taking their children out to a party and ignoring them, expecting someone else to do their childcare until it goes wrong. Have you ever walked down the pavement toward an idiot who is more interested in looking at their phone, head buried in the screen, rather than looking where they are going; or they stroll across the road in front of traffic without looking, while the poor motorist tries to dodge them? Yep, that's generation numpty Zda's or Zda+, a walking, not talking, health and safety risk to the public. Whilst social media and the smart phone technology can be used for positive outcomes, there is an increase in the number of anti-social numpty Z generation. Like armchair warriors who post vile bullying messages online, technology is another excuse for people's irresponsibility or unaccountability for their place in general society.

So where does this leave the UK? We currently have a conquest on our hands in the form of mass illegal immigration and drug culture in every town/city. We wage war on each other in the form of violent protests based upon disagreement, lack of free speech and violent crime 'citizen on citizen'. Death is an easy one - stabbing, especially the youth, and murder in general are on the up and has been due to the lack of attention from the political system. Famine -a record number of people using food banks and having to make a choice between heating or eating, and whilst there is a large contingent of brazen shoplifters who steal to raise funds for their drug habit, many shoplifters do it to put food on the table. The impact on society of generation Z+ has many more years to playout, the question is will it be better or worse? I suspect we know the answer already.

Patriotism Not Allowed

A definition of patriotism, and there are many, relates to you loving, supporting and defending your country, what made it great, the history, culture and where you came from. So being patriotic is a positive thing. A way of identifying with it can be a national flag or supporting something that represents your country, for example, an Olympic team; the Lionesses; England rugby team; scientists creating the Covid vaccine and the Union Jack Flag. Being proud of what has been achieved in the name of your country is to be patriotic.

Whilst Kier and Rishi may talk the talk, they don't want you to be patriotic. It's clear that they don't walk the talk, far from it. Their mantra and focus are completely the opposite. Yes, they have allowed our history and achievements as a country to be diluted. Their gaze is apparently on everything but the UK, appeasing the lefties as they tear down historical statues and vandalise whatever stands in their way. Whether we like it or not history is history and cannot and should not be re-shaped or forgotten. We should learn from our past mistakes and not repeat them but continue with the good things. What people need to rationalise is that if there is a symbol/reminder of something they believe to be bad, inevitably it acts as a reminder that we should not repeat it. For example, World War II (1939), Vietnam (1955). War is equal to Death. This is bad. It translates to millions of people suffering and dying. There are many symbols across the world marking respect for the people that gave their lives to defeat the Nazi war machine, less so for the veterans of Nam. The lessons are obvious; avoid war if possible; try to come to an agreement and maintain peace. If that fails be very ready for any threat to our way of life, or at worst be ready for war?

It's the last clause of the previous sentence which the UK establishment has missed since the Thatcher days. We have seen the political elite wade in on this or that summit, Gaza, the Ukraine. The UK takes the moral high ground, putting itself forward as a peacekeeper. To have any effect or sway with the aggressor you must have clout or be a threat. In military language this means you have a bigger stick (arsenal) than the other guy and he will listen to you. So, considering where the UK stands at the moment against most of the wars, we couldn't scare an ant. If the cuffs came off and we were attacked or invaded, would we have much of a chance? No. Our only plausible option would probably be nuclear and nobody of a sane mind wants that, not even Putin. Therefore, to demonstrate the political elite's level of patriotism, I put this to you:

Even since the Iraq war the level of investment in the UK military has been very low. I suspect the attitude is that it has all gone quiet so why invest? Is their equipment up to muster? The number of Armed Forces personnel has declined significantly according to the ukdefencejournal.org.uk (30/5/24), in fact by a third in the last 23 years (forcesnews.com 29/1/24). Overall spending has increased but by nowhere near enough as was pointed out by President Trump. Fair play for Kier pledging more cash for defence, but it was not given willingly. Let's not forget who twisted Kier's and Nato's arm (Trump) into coughing up a bit more. It's too little too late really. If a military threat came along tomorrow - no country could mobilise that quickly, it needs forethought and planning. I am not a rocket scientist but if I can read and watch international developments and quickly interpret that the world has become more war hungry in the last 2-3 years, then the obvious question is, what have the UK government and advisers been doing? Probably the EDI training. Being patriotic would have meant that you would have focussed more on defence in peace times, to be ready for the threats as they surface. In our present state, by the time the threat hits the UK, it would be too late.

There are currently 2100 (approx) military veterans who are homeless in the UK (AOAV.Org Dec 2023). These are the individuals who put their lives on the line when asked to. I would imagine that there are many from the Afghanistan conflict. This number is perhaps small in relation to the overall number of military personnel, but in my opinion the number is far too high. It would surely be nearer zero if we had a patriotic government.

These individuals have served this country and even risked their life for it. However, I'm not aware of them being treated to hotel accommodation and three meals a day like the illegals who have given this country nothing but a problem. Also, why are all current service personnel not allowed to wear their uniform in public unless it's a formal pre-arranged event? Apparently, it upsets/offends certain minorities who enjoy benefits and freedoms in the UK. In my opinion that's tough. What a disgrace. Everyone should respect the military. Who decided this ridiculous rule – I wonder? If there is an internal threat to our military that is of extreme concern, that threat should be removed from the UK. I am sure the government knows the threat and the people posing it! Military personnel and their families should receive recognition and be celebrated more often. In the USA recognition is given at every sport and entertainment event, veterans from the US (and often the UK) are asked to stand and they are thanked for the service they provide in helping to keep the US safe. They are applauded by the audience - that feels, looks and sounds like patriotism to me.

Homeland Security is as important as the external threats, not military personnel but a robust system, law and order force to protect every access point to the UK. The risk to our safety via our own borders must be of paramount concern. Surely, one of the easiest things to do when you're a small island is to defend your borders. The water around the UK has and continues to be a natural barrier; team this with a set of well managed border and military services and it should dissuade most attempts by anyone to invade. However, that does not seem to be the case, does it? I have already covered how easy it is to just jump off the water taxi from France and enter the UK without any challenge. Then there was the sacking of David Neil, the Chief Inspector of Borders and Immigration (in 2024) who clearly had concerns about security across our borders. Since leaving the EU, the borders at our airports and ports should have been changed in favour of the citizens of our country. – Yes, putting the UK citizens first. Many other countries prioritise their own citizens, how patriotic. I am a fairly well travelled individual. Whilst travelling by air is now one of the most overrated forms of travel, it is simply painful; queue to go through customs; queue to go through the flight gate and queue to board the plane and then repeat the whole process when you land at the other end. The borders at the major airports are in a disgraceful state. It's not just the long queues to re-enter your own country, or even the poor passenger management you experience. It's the general attitude and demeanour of the people who sit behind the desks and ask to see your passport. I have had many mixed experiences when returning to my own country. I have been made to feel like a criminal when not able to use the electronic E gates. I have witnessed many people of different nationalities and their extended families simply being waved through. It does beg the national security question. I did ask the border force person behind the desk at London Heathrow once as to why these non-nationals were being waved through, the response shocked and surprised me. He said, "Is there a problem sir? If you continue to question me, I will have you arrested and detained, it's not your concern what I do." I promptly stopped asking questions and went on my way. The real challenge I have is why is there not a UK only lane? Why should I have to queue with Europeans when we are no longer part of the Europe? It's totally backward thinking and an appalling way to treat your own citizens. We should have a system like the USA or some of the African countries, where their own citizens are welcomed back and prioritised over everyone else.

At a glance then, it appears that patriotism in the UK is slowly but surely being undermined by the very people who should be celebrating and fostering the good attributes of being British – the politicians-the owners of the pillars. What we have is the political elite dipping their heads, getting on their knees and apologising for it - disgraceful. Just like the lack of ambition for

Brexit and everything else. What we have is mediocrity and left-wing ideology to replace it.

One last thought and it has been debated many times - If the Union Jack flag is a representation of our (UK) country, culture and what we stand for, why it is not illegal to burn it or deface it?

Gamblers Always Tell You When They Win, Never How Much They Wasted!

The Winner of the 2024 General Election was?

Labour did win in 2024 and now we have probably the most hypocritical, half-truth, leftwing socialist government of all time in number 10. Yes, Kier and his party KierCo have emerged. To put it in perspective there was no 'real' majority, let's not forget the facts. The facts are, that only 20 % of eligible voters actually voted so we can hardly say that they are deserving of their place in power or say the British public gave us the mandate. Viewing it another way 80% of the voting public did not vote Labour. The real statistic which Labour hate is that only 1 in 5 people voted for them. Perhaps that's why it's so difficult to find a Labour supporter unless you are in an over-populated inner city; working in a public sector environment like a financially broken council or NHS trust; or maybe working in a heavily unionised employment. The clear loser of the 2024 election is the UK itself and the majority of people that live here and did not vote (the 4 in 5 voters), but that's on us. The UK under Keir and his cabinet (KeirCo) is simply a fast-track pass from the gutter to the sewer. The future state of the UK can be predicted but you may want to close your eyes and not read on.

New Kid on The Block

Now that Kier is Prime Minister, it will be interesting to see how he copes long-term. The 12–18-month honeymoon period will pass, and he will go from 'hero to zero' quickly, (although not quite as quick as Liz Truss or Theresa May). Even after 12 weeks in the seat he looked like a tortured man, nearly a year on and not much has changed, if anything he looks more confused than ever. It's only an observation but he seems awkward and uneasy in his own skin. What he appears to dislike is that no one, including the public or the media, are accepting of his consistent deflection and mis-direction game. His messaging and delivery seem plastic/artificial and insincere. This is a surprise after he had so much voice coaching during Covid, but I probably shouldn't say too much about that as I might end up in court. Sarah Vine of the Mail (24th Jan 2024) compared him to a vegan sausage roll, that's a bit far Sarah, I suspect that even a vegan sausage roll has taste! Keir, like Sadiq – blames everyone else, rather than leading from the front and being accountable for his poor decision-making, we will witness a lot more of the same as we go through the next four years to the election. It has been ascertained that Keir seems to prefer the Muslim community, (which is absolutely fine as many are British citizens), over the Christian/patriotic indigenous population of the UK. He clearly isn't patriotic as I have established. The Evening Standard (online 4/3/25), ran an article on Kier's attendance to observe Ramadan. He claimed that the British Muslim community had had a tough time (just like everyone in the UK since Covid, and indeed in the short time he has been in office) and hatred towards British Muslims was whipped up by the far-right rhetoric and disinformation particularly as a result of the Southport murders and riots in 2024. Yes, those same riots that I saw on tv several times in which gangs of young Asian men were trying to confront and agitate the situation. What happened to them? As for disinformation, well, we found out the real motive of the killer and what he was up to, but only many months after the police raided Rudakubana's home. I am not surprised but absolutely sure that it didn't take our trustworthy police that many months to determine the real facts or his motives. Meanwhile the riots continued spreading and Kier continued using inflammatory language. Jonathan Hall KC, the independent reviewer of Terrorism Legislation suggests (reported by GB News online 6/3/25) that withholding information is far more prejudicial than making the facts public knowledge. Hall, writing for The Telegraph said that the failing of the authorities to tell/release the facts in essence fuelled the disinformation and the riots. Furthermore, Merseyside Chief Constable Serene Kennedy admitted the authorities were instructed to conceal key details – even his religion? I wonder if the statement the authorities were going to release read 'UK citizen of Christian religion'. I still haven't worked out why there are concrete barricades on every main pedestrian foot path across most of the bridges in the City of London, what are they protecting us from?

It would appear then that Kier kept the real facts of the wanna be terrorist, (with an unknown religion for the first 3 months) from the public. Why? I ask; is it because he is a lawyer? Or ex-head of the CPS (whilst Jimmy Saville got off)? He is fully aware of the law and the corrupt system that supports it. My suggestion is a simple one; Keir used the riots to promote his anti 'far left' agenda and blame the far right to fuel the fire and keep the riots bubbling, then fast-track everyone and anyone remotely involved to our already oversubscribed prisons. Or maybe it was just redirecting the noise from more embarrassment of the so-called and made up £22bn debt that Rachel in accounts harps on about. "A cunning plan master" (Kier), Baldrick would say in Black Adder (BBC TV program in the eighties). His latest magic trick, which failed spectacularly, was calling parliament back in to save British Steel from the Chinese firm Jingye. This could have clearly been done weeks/months before." No" says Keir. Lights, camera, action, let's try and cover up more embarrassment and continued U-turns, like having to water down the child abuse (grooming gangs) review; or the U-turn on green spending and probably more likely the growing list of blunders from Rach in accounts as his chancellor. And if you think that's low, Keir suggests that the good people of the UK need to take back the Union Jack flag from the far right and protect the values of our country, wow- a cheap and amateur attempt for Kier at being a nationalist.

The desperation is starting to set in. His position is clear. For a man who has previously described himself as quietly patriotic, Kier's thought process is, "I am losing seats to Nigel (Reform) so I will bash and have a dig at the Right and try and win back the middle ground voters) suggesting to us he is very patriotic and cares about the UK and its culture – what nonsense. Action always speaks louder than words. Going back to Europe and grovelling to be back on the corrupt European parliament (the independent auditors still haven't signed off their accounts); failing to stop the economic and cultural bombshell of illegal immigration or failing to invest in our Military to protect us in this very uncertain world in which we find ourselves. I beg to differ Kier; you are merely deflecting/showboating. It's not a game, it's a country and its future looks bleaker than ever with you attempting to run it.

Another 'cunning plan' which he thinks we have missed, is the language he used in his acceptance speech. In summary he had a mandate, and he would look after the voters who gave him the mandate (remember the 1- in- 5 voters). In simple terms this is what he is doing, sod the rest of the country (that's 4 out of 5 voters) it seems. KeirCo will help and do pretty much anything for the people who will vote for them, he wants to appease the folk in the inner cities with high levels of minorities and areas with high levels of public services (NHS, big University cities). Why has he done little to stop the small (getting larger by the day) boats? You may ask. Well, every new boatload is more votes for Labour, and I am sure they will be next in line to get a vote like the 16-year-olds have. Back to Blair and Brown tactics with open immigration policy. Who doesn't vote for Labour, pensioners; farmers; private sector industry workers; Northeast and Southeast England. Look how he has helped these areas since he has been in power, enough said. It's not often you see tractors in Westminster, banners on bridges and in fields, at the side of motorways telling us that Labour have broken their promises and done a dirty on the farmers.

The cracks will start to appear as the economic and social impact introduced by KeirCo begin to be felt by the general public. The popularity rating will hit rock bottom after about a year to 18 months for this weak leader. The media will have a field day about all the crack-pot nonsense KierCo has started to come out with. Like the waste of many billions for Ed Miliband's net zero project which has no real prospect of providing cheaper or better supply of energy for businesses/households. Or tax rise after tax rise despite promises not to do so from Rach, the first 'female' chancellor. I wouldn't care if she was an alien – just do your job well and stop trying to spook the public and industry. The economy takes about 12-18 months to properly adjust in general terms, to policy/law changes/budgetary factors; however, the social impact can be almost instant when a politician opens their mouth before engaging their brain, which tends to happen often. The six mistakes that will secure Kier's demise, maybe more, as we move into the final quarter of 2025 are:

> **Stabbing in Southport** – After the deliberate and calculated attack on a school in Southport in 2024, a stabbing of young children and teachers resulting in three pointless deaths, a number of people became upset and took to the streets in protest – rightly so. How on earth can this happen on the streets of the UK, a mad man running amok around a school, stabbing children? Unfortunately, after the initial peaceful protest, the thugs felt the need to join in and riots started, quickly escalating out of hand. At this point we started to see the real Keir. Not a Prime Minister or Statesman, no, more like an attorney general/lawyer. Rather than asking for calm and unity initially, he chose inflammatory gung-ho language, which only angered the public and the thugs further. Consequently, we know how that ended.

Lack of a plan to address illegal immigration -Keir had seen the numbers; read the newspapers; watched the news and clearly understood, (or so you would have thought), that immigration is a massive issue. Yet he came to the table without a plan to attempt to slow it down, or even better, end it completely. Numbers will significantly increase under Labour. KeirCo declared war on the smugglers, made a few tweaks to the law and blurted profuse hot air like the governments before them. I have said enough on the illegals coming to the UK previously, but labour will break one record, and that is a whopping increase in the overall numbers. More will be allowed to stay, damaging the UK economy and culture to a far greater extent than any other government has managed in UK history. KeirCo failing to set targets on immigration, is a very clear signal (and they know it) that the measures they have put in place are simply window dressing, a facade and will not work. The way I see it is that, if a Prime Minister fails to set a target/and or stop the illegals it should be treated as treason in my mind. It's simply failing to protect the country's economy, the State, and the safety of the people. Failure to make the right decision and stop or deal correctly with the illegals is a deliberate betrayal of this country. In May 2025 a Labour official, Dan Jarvis stands up in the commons and talks about the need for more tools and resources to address the ongoing and increased threats to the State, the majority backed by Iran, very worrying that. Dan boldly states that "Government will not hesitate to act in a robust manner to threats", which is commendable but what about the elephant in the room, I ask? The elephant being the threat (economical, cultural, potential terrorist) that arrives every day from across the channel- thousands of war-age men with no identity. Dan and his team clearly need to expand their focus.

Illegal immigration is and will remain the biggest issue for the next 10-15 years unless it is dealt with promptly and there is no faith that KierCo will deal with it effectively or efficiently from a cost perspective, just more taxpayers' money for the French. Increasingly Keir will look to call out and/or criminalise anyone who disagrees on immigration as Far Right or Racism. This deliberate lack of objectivity and ability to understand the publics' views on immigration is simply killing free speech and expression; driving divide in our society and people become steadily angrier. We have seen examples surface, and the true colours shine though from KierCo on other topics, suggesting that; anyone calling for an inquiry into the grooming gangs scandal, for example, is a far-right activist (GB news 6/1/25)

The caving-in to the unions - Unions will keep coming back for more, the proverbial Oliver Twist. History often repeats itself and Labour will cave in. Whether it's through the trains, NHS, Whitehall cronies or bin men. Labour councils and bin men and women have had fun before in the late 1970s, now we have the same trouble with the bankrupt, obviously incompetent councils. More of this behaviour will follow.

War on the pensioners - A pathetic show of disregard and arrogance in removing the winter fuel allowance. Let's help save money, namely, rob the people that need it most. Who dreamt that one up? £1.4bn saving (apparently if you believe Rach's numbers, does anyone?). You could save 6 times that by not pandering to the public sector unions' demands in the first couple of days of being in office. How about sorting out the EDI and management across the public sector saving probably around 3 or 4 times what they took off the pensioners. Their pensions will be next, tax, tax and more tax, with means-testing to follow. It's easy to rob the old folk, there was no difficult decision made there. What would be difficult, is to show some strategic thinking and take a good look at your own house and get that in order.

Asian Grooming Gangs – nothing to answer apparently
- Before I get started let's call this grooming label what it is 'Child Sex Abuse'. The British public know it and are sick of the establishment trying to smoke screen and cover their embarrassment in not acting/dealing with the problem. That's the people who are doing this disgusting act and the culture that promotes it. KierCo has a great opportunity to show leadership in this space. In hindsight, the Tories were pitiful and KierCo is following the same path. How about, taking the victims seriously, and lock up/deport these sick individuals out of our society? They have no place here. This subject has been kicking about for a long time, years in fact, from the dodgy Tony days, and Keir's now involved. The government and authorities have done little to thwart this unlawful behaviour, which appears to be Asian related, (according to GB News). It's a despicable set of circumstances on the streets of the UK. It's not uncommon to witness a complete lack of intervention from the authorities/ government. We have all seen the failing to address the drug problem, knife crime and cultural indifference that this country struggles with, time and again. I am not a fan of public inquiries as they do little to improve things. They lack consequence for the wrong-doers; many should be treated as criminals. It's rather like lessons learned in a corporate context, but nothing really changes; the people responsible for the failings never lose their job or get prosecuted. Yes, but look, we spent a lot of taxpayer's money and have a piece of paper with some stuff written on it. However, none of this really matters in the context of having or not having

a public inquiry for KeirCo. The tipping point was the abstinence, arrogance and reluctance to acknowledge it and pass it off as nothing, like shit on their shoe. A leader would have considered the mood of the country; have a moral compass to do the right thing; less so the media, but more importantly considered the victims rather than the perpetrators. Finally, the quangos have woken up and advised KeirCo it's morally wrong to do something under the radar and buy some time. Aha! an ethnicity inquiry, yep that will do the job and fend off the people/media until the next shiny thing comes along? But no one is buying it Keir, it's all total BS from Labour and the Conservatives before them. Simon Danczuk a labour MP for Rochdale (2010-2017), critically sums up the, "Cowardice, snobbery and blind-eyed culture and attitude of government and the authorities in dealing with the disgraceful act." Daily Mail (13th Jan 2025). Simon highlights consistent failures of the authorities. Is this really how we deal with child sex abuse in the UK?

Bending over for the EU - It would appear that Kier is light on friends, despite his travel bill and cosying up to anyone from anywhere. He loves to get on his knees in order to win political friendship. It's no surprise that (now) this new self-acclaimed patriot who wants to save the Union Jack flag and the values it stands for, is happy to sell his soul and our lives to the corrupt, unelected European Government. Clearly, he is a remoaner/remainer like most of the politicians in Westminster. Kier's European Reset is the open door for Europe to control the UK and bleed us dry of any wealth we have left, and that won't be much by the time Labour finishes their term. Just looking at the basics of the reset, a 5-year-old child could probably tell you how one-sided and ridiculously in favour it is for the EU. Keir get off your knees and lead, don't grovel! In summary, we must abide by their laws and rules; let their fishermen destroy our already overfished coastline; allow cheaper student fees for their youth, midway, we have some information sharing, but what's in it for us? Well, we don't have to queue at the airports in Europe anymore. Wow, what a dealmaker he is!

My opinion of Keir has changed from the view I had pre 2024 election, not for the better I might add, he is clearly in the **spineless** territory. From what I see now, he is a one-trick pony, a lawyer, and he is trying to run the country like the CPS. Many would claim he did a bad job of that. As time has passed and things have come to light that we did not see first time around, the new kid on the block clearly does not have the experience or leadership needed; he does not understand or want to understand the real issues facing this country, just his own agenda. So rather than burn taxpayers' money and take, take, take, *au contraire,* give us something back, and drop the left-wing ideology. I suspect both the arrogance and ignorance will continue as KierCo lie to themselves and pass off their poorly thought-through ideas for the next big shiny thing that catches their eye, (magpie characteristics). Keir will continue to blame everyone else for his poor decisions. I suspect that is another motivation for him to bend over for the EU. I can hear it now, "It was a mandate from the EU, nothing to do with me, that mess."

Kier's behaviour further demonstrates that he is not a leader nor nationalist. He is simply a lawyer who is out of touch and out of his depth floundering. Watching him on occasions at PM question time he is rude and petulant like a school bully, and it won't be long before (metaphorically speaking, not wanting to incite violence and end up in prison) someone punches him on the nose and stops him. It will not be long before you're done Kier.

The media will continue to get noisy with Keir and his arrogant KierCo mob, rightly so, calling out the blatant contradictions, U-turns and lies, which started to appear in just weeks of them getting into power. His party like the Conservatives in the last 10 years will turn on each other. Kier will start to falter, the knives will come out, I suspect he may not last the full term. Probably 12-24 months tops. Then the socialist left-wing labour donors and unionists will get what they really wanted in the first place, namely, loudmouth Angela. She may have gone (in the most spurious set of circumstances), but she will be back. Well, we all know what will happen then, to call it catastrophic would be an understatement. Maybe an early election.

A Little Comment About Brexit

Well, it was a huge opportunity for the UK. Many of those in Westminster were never fully behind it. I wonder how many politicians and privileged lords have holiday homes in Europe and enjoyed working from home, by just popping off to Europe under the radar. Given the cost and levels of interest in Brexit, whilst the vote was close, we live in a democracy. and the vote was the vote. A majority said leave and prosper, but then you had the spoilt brat remainers, many of whom, refused to accept the vote and participate. No, the remainers just started crying like babies, throwing their dummies out of their prams, and trying to de-rail any form of progress. If the politicians and Whitehall cronies had embraced it and followed through on the will of the voting public (the majority), Brexit really could have propelled us to become a great nation again. The UK could have been admired by the world, for our grit, determination to defy the odds and above all, lead. But alas no, we did a few foreign deals, made some friends outside of Europe and decided it's all a bit tough (difficult as politicians say). Now, after that half-arsed attempt, it's been called a failure. The public should never have been given the vote – the public don't know or understand what they are voting for. How insulting I say! I refuse to accept that argument when the people/politicians using this narrative are the very reason why this country is in such a mess – oh and apparently, they are in charge of running this country? Brexit is now being used as a good excuse for Kier or Rishi before him to cosy up to the EU. Keir will get on his knees and sign us back up to an unelected government that does not favour the UK, appears to loathe it – unless we are handing over billions of pounds. As a result of poor leadership and political self-interest the Brexit opportunity has been wasted.

Julie Rothchild

You Really Cannot Teach This Old Dog New Tricks – Far Left?

Old Labour/New Labour/Just Labour = KeirCo

As I have outlined, behaviours are a key part of looking and being credible in front of the country and on the world stage. But is Kier on top of his team? We have seen inflammatory, racist, insightful behaviour, fake News from this Labour party. Surely conviction and prison should follow. We have been here before with other Labour Governments, but now we have the emergence of KeirCo. Will things be any different? KeirCo have been an opposition party for many years so have had an opportunity to learn the right and wrong ways of conducting themselves – you'd think? Not only that, but what have they learned since Jeremy Corbyn and the then labour party broke the law due to their appalling 2016-2020 row regarding Anti-Semitism? Clearly not much. There will be double standards and more u-turns than the average American road system. KeirCo will probably go down as the most hated party in British politics, not that that's a very high standard as I have outlined in this book. Let's look at the behaviour of the KierCo mob, since forming their amateur dramatic political team:

Dawn Butler – The well-known extreme left-wing antagonist calls the new leader of the Conservatives, Kemi Badenoch, a black faced white supremist in a vile racist attack (Evening Standard 2024). Sounds like a woman who is jealous that Kemi has achieved so much in a short time, sounds like Dawn has been a bit of an underperformer in her political career, maybe? Just shouting stuff out to grab a headline.

Kier Starmer – in June 2025 suggested that the UK is an island of strangers. What a bizarre thing to say, when you as PM should be trying to lead the people and provide a sense of unity given the current woes and divide. It's a bit like the Union Jack and his ill-placed comments after the Southport murders regarding the yobbery. His comments, so un-natural, more lawyer like, experienced leaders and statesmen do not talk this type of narrative – come on Kier, stop reading what everyone tells you to say, I am sure Sadiq is involved in the scripting somewhere?

Ricky Jones – Calling for right wing protesters on a march in London for their 'throats to be cut'. He has been charged and has pleaded not guilty. Obviously, just a slip of the tongue. I am sure he will receive the same treatment and fate as the Southport rioters, right? Inflammatory posturing and inciting violence it looked like to me, yet his trial was delayed until August 2025, and I am sure he will get a slapped hand like Mike Amesbury.

David Lammy – Comparing Trump to Hitler is either radical, stupid or just plain hatred. Clearly saying 'Trump is not only a woman-hating, Neo-Nazi; he is a profound threat to international order' David sounds like a scared man, deflecting responsibility away from his own incompetence as a Foreign Secretary. Now Trump is in power, it will be interesting to see how long he can last. It is funny though how an apparently responsible politician is happy to try and look tough in front of his peers, and now looks like a complete Duffus, and to pass it off as old news, just shows total arrogance. David Lammy is clearly more interested in woke virtue signalled by flying the EDI flags over foreign office in Sept 24 rather than carrying out the duties and priorities of looking out for the country in very unstable and uncertain times. Or perhaps he thinks that the Ukraine War and Gazza conflict are fake news, and climate change is real because it rained a lot this year in the UK? Trump will have fun with this one, but like all great leaders I am sure he will sort and put his country first before having fun with Lammy.

Mike Amesbury – assaulted a member of the public in Cheshire in October 2024 whilst being a member of parliament for Labour. Common assault apparently? Look at the CCTV footage (Thanks to the Mirror online 2024) it seemed a little more severe than common assault. Maybe not due to the man's injuries but the fact he carried on hitting the man whilst he was on the ground, that feels a bit more like 'intent' to cause further injuries. There are people serving prison sentences for 3-5 years for such an offence, but the CPS and the judge decided he could get away with 10 weeks. After making a further plea he served 3 nights in jail and a suspended sentence. Lucky Mike.

It's fair to say that we will see more, much more of this from Labour as they continue to underperform for the country and erode trust in politics. Weren't Labour supposed to restore trust in politics? They are not off to a great start. are they?

The lefties run off crying – Trump effect

There is no doubt that American citizens turned out in their millions to vote in the Trump vs Kamala 2024 election. Having spent some time in Texas, Florida, Kansas and California, their voting dilemma is not very different from the UK - Good, Bad or Spineless. Whilst the 2024 election in the UK had a low turnout, largely due to disgruntled Tory voters wanting to teach their own party a lesson (rightly so), the turn out in the American election was very different in overall numbers circa 140m. Politics and the policies set in the USA are very evident in the majority of the citizens day to day life. A deterioration of living standards; massive increases in fuel and food costs; crime on the increase; personal debt out of control; corrupt authorities; a broken justice system; more and more people in poverty; and a reduction in public service, not that there are many - sound familiar? It's a left-wing mediocrity, zombie outbreak that the majority of weak western world has succumbed to. The woke agenda has sneaked up on us over the last 20 years with the promises of benefits, but the results are unrest, prejudice, unhappiness and debt. However, the battle ground left wing Democrats vs right wing Republicans is like Labour Vs Conservatives of old- 10-20 years ago. Simply put the privileged elite and celebrity town who voted left (Kamala) and the real working citizens and business owners who voted right (Trump).

Trump's win will be good for America, because it will focus on helping American tax paying, citizens who have struggled under the Biden administration. Trump promotes ambition and success over being on the world stage or just grabbing headlines and delivering little. Personally, whilst not liking his personal style so much, as a leader and president he really is the man for the job. He will get stuff sorted, aligning the economy, national security and above all the biggest threat to the west the illegal immigration pandemic in the form of strong border control. I am a fan of that. How refreshing would it be to have a UK leader who had the same agenda and focussed on the majority of people in the UK rather than left-wing ideology.

The most interesting reaction which supports my claim of why the left socialist outlook in the UK (and anywhere else for that matter) is wrong is the scare mongering and negative personal messaging from the lefties in relation to Trump's victory i.e Ed Davy, Carla Denyer amongst others running scared with no backbone. Posting personal dislike rather than seeing Donald's appointment as positive, an opportunity to benefit our relationship and the country in terms of trade – the tariffs rhetoric had us worried. Perhaps it's just another way to grab a headline and try to keep their agenda's going. Of course, before election the Labour lefties from 2017 to date have a string of personal criticism towards Trump; this further supports my argument that Labour are inexperienced and conduct student union politics. The Daily Express (Jan 2025) ran a great article outlining the personal insults KierCo have given, as they try and look like they mean business and tough political opponents. Boy, has this backfired to the detriment of the UK as we will be placed towards the back of the list when it comes to US trade deal? The elitist arrogance of the KierCo shines so brightly, it's alright saying Trump and Elon should not interfere in our politics but is it ok to spend taxpayers' money sending Labour cronies to the US to interfere in their game of political chess supporting Kamala. The impact of the so-called Labour interference was hardly mentioned on US TV. That is because the cronies don't understand the complexity of a free market or for that matter American democracy. Being in California at this time was a priceless experience to witness what you don't see in the UK. Trump was going to win; it was so obvious.

Then came the Inauguration and I witnessed a true and measured leader, (more so this time round) who had learned the US political lessons from his previous stint. Leaders do not waste time whingeing and whining about the past and the hand they have been dealt over and over again for months and months, like we witness daily from KierCo. No, a leader acknowledges it and immediately sets out plans to address it because he has read the mood of his country. How refreshing that he wants to challenge the status quo which, has left the USA in a crisis on many fronts. Citing illegal Immigration, Woke as a very damaging impact on American society – too right. He wants to strengthen the military given the uncertainty in the world and jettison left-wing ideology to give Americans more jobs and money in their pockets. Trump as a leader does not accept the status quo when it is damaging and hurting Americans. Trump is a tad right wing and a patriot who takes action. However, I did laugh very loud when no one from the Labour party got the usual customary invitation to the inauguration. it was hardly surprising when all of KierCo slagged him off, calling him a racist, misogynist, an imbecile and belligerent, to name but a few insults. The two I read in disbelief was Jonathan Reynolds a clear remoaner (Business Secretary) 'Disregards all but himself – Like Brexiteers' and Ed Miliband

'A misogynistic, self-confessed groper' according to the Daily Mail (9/11/24). Wow, it really sums up the talent in the Labour Camp. They sure know how to win people over and promote international trade. Well Trump is here, so it will be an interesting time for our so-called special relationship.

The future is about opportunity, something to look forward to because we have learned from our history and previous mistakes

The UK's future State

You probably thought that I was going to start this section being positive and suggesting that life under Labour will improve. Sorry. Well, under Labour things are going to become a lot worse, wait and see. No, it really won't take long before we see how bad things are going to get along with the chaos, both socially and economically. From day one I have witnessed student union politics one on one. I have read the book, passed the exam, never had a real job in the real world before and now Labour/KierCo are running the country. Their whole way of going about it is amateur and dangerous for the UK. If you voted Labour and you're already fed up (if not, you will be soon) then that's on you; give yourself a pat on the back. I didn't and never would vote for this crowd of elitist, far left-wing idiots. They never have learned anything from the past, they simply repeat the same mistakes, dream up the sound bites, making promises they know themselves they cannot keep. Underneath the rhetoric, it's the same old story just dressed up differently. As my mother would say 'mutton dressed as Lamb' in every way.

Labour have already started to blame the previous conservative government for everything, which is standard practice so nothing new there. The economy is worse than expected; we will have to make some, wait for it, 'difficult decisions' due to very difficult situations; we are both socially and economically in trouble as a result of the Tories, so whatever happens is not our fault. Please spare us from these political oxygen thieves prattling on. For many years as the opposition, Labour have shouted, disrupted, bad mouthed pretty much every policy put forward by the conservatives, now the shoe is on the other foot. KierCo need to stop moaning and get on with the job they are paid to do, which remember they so eagerly wanted to show us how good they were pre-election. Well now you have it KeirCo, fill your boots, crack on, it's time to put big boy pants on and do the job. Whining for a couple of weeks is ok, but beyond that everyone can see you have no substance, no idea. The same poor excuses for their bad decision-making embarrassment cover up tactics will be deployed to keep them in power for as long as possible. It's fair to say KierCo have not had a great start 150 days in. Or have certain events played into their divisive hands to promote more left-wing ideology and deflection opportunities helped them to cover up their mistakes? This behaviour will continue and there is more to come. We will perhaps see the passing of laws to ban anything that objects to or does not agree with the KeirCo agenda. Another example, his attack on Reform (apparently Far Right) could he try and ban the party or its leader Nigal Farage or GB News? (great watch by the way); maybe 'Have I Got News for you'; maybe 'Private Eye'. How about anyone that has anything bad to say about immigration – what nonsense I hear you say? No, I say, KeirCo is a danger to democracy, free speech and anything that is mildly British or for that matter patriotic. They could bring in special legal and sentencing measures to stop only certain groups of protesters or criminals who are apparently far right that threaten the state as they acted on fake news, oh, he has already done that! This type of political behaviour is very divisive; they will claim - subjective. It's so obviously personal rather than considered in a wider context of what is happening in the UK. But if you're far left you can be vile, offensive and bend the rules as Ross Clark pointed out in the Daily Mail (22/12/22) and we all know left wing thuggery like Stop Racism, who turn up and goad individuals peacefully demonstrating against asylum hotels into defending themselves (Epping what happened there?). It would appear that intimidation, goading and antagonising is ok, but if you react to it, its unlawful.

Before going to print (Oct 2025) KierCo are already starting to fix things to save their embarrassment for their student union politics and bad decision making. The attempt to merge local councils' devolution/ revolution scheme feels like a deliberate attempt to delay the number of May 2025 local council elections which if they go ahead in totality will see Labour annihilated. So let's pretend, make something up. Let's learn from the disaster that was the Greater London Council experience. There is no promise of savings or promise of better social services. Many councils mostly Labour can't even balance their books or provide adequate social service. Joining them together is just more red tape, state jobs and bureaucracy, that's not exactly streamlining costs, it will simply increase them. No. It's just about saving face and delaying the inevitable for Kier as leader in the short term. What is even worse is the Conservative run councils also jumping on the band wagon to save their embarrassment too, do they have no moral or democratic compass? We will see more and more of these silly ideas, schemes with no structure, clear governance or plan to implement them. Just saying things are going to happen because I said so does not make them happen KeirCo, It merely shows they are following the current trend in politics; lack of common sense; little experience; poor acumen and zero moral judgement. Under normal guidelines the devolution/revolution would have been seen for what it is- Bribery and Corruption, but because we are politicians saying stuff - it's ok, trust us.

On a more and very dangerous footing, the UK is heading towards a Total Surveillance State. One must question the sanity of the decision makers implementing this wholesale on its own citizens, rather than targeting criminals and illegals. George Orwell's book 1984 is not conceptually far from what Labour is introducing now, however this is not merely a dystopian work of fiction, this, quite disturbingly is our dystopian reality. Let me join up the dots for you:

Technology – The Online Services Act, to use anything deemed slightly adult or political in content you must provide personal information. What you do on the internet will be recorded (forever) against your identity. Add a slice of Digital ID cards, which have even more personal information about you, and you will have to enter your details before accessing any form of online content, again everything links back to your ID.' What follows next?' you ask. Well, Labour with support from the financial institutions and big retailers could remove cash and make all transactions digital. Add a splash of ANPR. The culmination of this technology cocktail means the government of the day owns you and every movement you make.

Trust - by far the biggest question to ask is who owns and looks after the data? What controls and governance are in place to protect it? What are your rights? So, the real issue is do you trust the government and its affiliates with your data? I suspect I know the answer. The collection and misuse of data is a big problem for the public, under a totalitarian leader. Manipulation of the truth; propaganda and suppression of the individual, tend to follow. Surely that can't be the UK in the now/future?

And if that's not bad enough what about the hackers, perhaps Labour will recruit the Technology and Cyber Security lead from Jaguar to help implement it?

The public are so fed up with this type of rubbish, I am sure we will see more new and very interesting laws from KeirCo to protect their left-wing ideology.

In short; unemployment will go up; tax will increase on every level; the economy will stagnate; cultural erosion will increase; freedoms will be taken away; crime will hit an all-time high; there will be significant unrest as a result of illegal immigration as the numbers sky rocket; the unions will have more strikes, the bloating will continue in the public sector. So, the pillars of society are cracking! Let's hope the next four years pass by quickly and we can vote for something different because real correction will be needed. KierCo will do so much damage to this country, the challenge to fix it will be almost impossible – I just hope, that whoever it is, they don't moan and prattle on about it like Labour have done.

Along Came Kemi

So, after the disaster of the 2024 elections KeirCo got in, Rishi stepped down or got pushed off the step he was sitting on, the race for a new conservative leader was on. There were some new faces and some of the usual suspects, but again it was difficult to spot a real leader that would inspire me to vote for them. The new leader will of course be the saviour of the party after the previous disasters. However, I suspect history will repeat itself, it will take several attempts and leaders to get the conservatives back as a leading party. The result came in, finally coming down to Badenoch and Jenrick, (sounds a bit like an eighties cop show) which one would be the leader? Both were unknown characters to me, but we learned more as the competition went on and both seemed evenly matched. My preference was Robert, but Kemi came out on top and became the leader of the Conservative party in November 2024. There is no doubt that she is bright and energised and as the months have gone on, I do not see her leading her party as a single united unit with clear vision. Her choice of cabinet was a bit weak and will need time to mature and get the right experience. Kemi has become more and more shouty, a bit like labour as the opposition. This is disappointing because I feel she has fallen for the classic tit for tat politics of noise over substance which voters are fed up with witnessing and simply change the channel. It is unlikely that she will stay the course to the next election. Will the Tories revert to their losing ways like doing their dirty washing in public and blatant sabotage of leaders from the shadows? Time will tell. Good luck Kemi.

Whilst the Conservatives currently hold the leader of the opposition title, as time passes the real challenger in the shape of Reform and Nigel will rise. I think we have passed the point where unhappy Tories protest vote has ended. They are gaining genuine interest as the only party that can help the UK come back from the last 20-30 years and the catastrophic mess labour will leave behind. However, it won't be that straight forward for Reform, as I have highlighted and there is clearly more to do before the next election.

Julie Rothchild

Nothing Will Get Better Unless Things Change – It's in Your Hands

Your Role – Take Action

There are many things you can and should do, protesting can but does not necessarily mean going out on the streets. It can be targeted, specific; have a moan you have earned the right! Remember it should be peaceful, measured and apply common sense. The action you take is important and it will ultimately change things, the biggest being at the next by-election or general election vote. Postal or in person VOTE. If you are online, sign up for the online petitions and sign/support them if we agree with the narrative (change.org). The next level down is the underperforming public departments, transport companies and other poor performing corporates, get complaining and share your experiences with your friends and family. Get your local councillor involved, that is what they are there for. Many of these departments and companies rely on a passive customers strategy and/or simply make it difficult for you to complain. If you have limited access to email or social media, put pen to paper and send them a letter. So, it's time for us, the UK citizens, to stop accepting shambolic below par services and behaviours and have your say.

Julie Rothchild

The voters are forgotten, while the political swine indulge themselves in personal interest and self-preservation – when's the next election?

Nobody

I hope you enjoyed the short version of my book, if so, I have achieved my objective to help you understand, simplifying the UK we live in today and where it's going wrong. I hope you now feel empowered to go and vote at the ballot box. Just remember it's us the public who decide what type of political animal represents us – who best represents your views now, aspirations for the future.

So, who am I and why should I take the time, effort and expense to write this book? In simple political terms, as I have outlined, I am Nobody, just a voter, the only interest politics gives me is when there is an election, every 4/5 years when they wheel out more fake promises than social media. I am in my late fifties I have a great family, I have worked, paid my taxes since the age of 16. I have been careful with my money, other than a mortgage, I have never bought anything I could not afford. I have worked for small, medium and global corporations and have vast business experience, life skills and a business degree, unlike many politicians of today! My view on life is simple; treat people how you want to be treated yourself. Respect and trust are the foundation of a good relationship but must be earned not given. Faith and hope are emotions that start within you but should not cloud your ability in judging the facts – tell it how it is and be honest. Never go looking for trouble, but if it comes to your door, deal with it as it is presented to you. Apply common sense to all situations.

On this basis, I am more than qualified and have a right to give my personal opinion and view on this country and the disgraceful state it's in, All thanks to bad and spineless politicians, and the so called leaders of all government departments, (Whitehall cronies) who have made a total and complete mess of this country over the last 30 years. The fact is I have paid these peoples' salary. I have followed the path to be a good citizen. Yet, the rabble in Westminster have consistently underperformed and not delivered on their promise. So, my view is valid, and I make no apology for giving it. The UK could have been a much better and more prosperous place to live in, than it is today.

Take 2

Vol 2 will focus on similar topics and again address what is needed to correct them. Not only do the government of the day own the pillars of our society, their influence and power trickles down to many other organisations, individuals and that's why leading and being a good example is so important. What we do have is the opposite and I will highlight some ugly unethical corporate behaviour; call out some additional government departments that need a complete re-think; comment on the left-wing crack-pot ideas Labour have been showboating and give my prediction on the winner of the next general election. I sincerely hope that KierCo have not been allowed to completely outlaw free speech, (although they are having a good go at it). Or Vol 2 won't make the bookshelf!

www.ingramcontent.com/pod-product-compliance
Lightning Source LLC
Chambersburg PA
CBHW071714020426
42333CB00017B/2271